When
Crisis
Comes

When
Crisis
T. Cecil Myers ~~~~~~~~~ Comes

ABINGDON PRESS
Nashville
New York

WHEN CRISIS COMES

Copyright © 1967 by Abingdon Press

Library of Congress Catalog Card Number: 67-14984

Scripture quotations labeled RSV are from the Revised Standard Version of the Bible, copyrighted 1946 and 1952 by the Division of Christian Education, National Council of Churches, and are used by permission.

Quotation on p. 13 is from Bayard Taylor's translation of *Faust,* published in *World's Great Plays,* and is used by permission of the World Publishing Company. Poem on p. 22 by John Oxenham is used by permission of Miss Theo Oxenham. Quotation on page 29 from *Back to Methuselah* by George Bernard Shaw is used by permission of The Public Trustee and The Society of Authors. Quotation on p. 32 from *The Cocktail Party* by T. S. Eliot is used by permission of Harcourt, Brace & World, Inc., and Faber & Faber, Ltd. Quotation on p. 55 from *The Age of Anxiety* by W. H. Auden, copyrighted 1947, is reprinted by permission of Random House, Inc. Poem on pp. 90-91 by Rolland W. Schloerb is used by permission of Mrs. Schloerb. Quotation on p. 96 is from "Transfusion," copyright by Paul Barrett, Music, Inc. Poem on p. 132 by Edwin Markham is reprinted by permission of Virgil Markham. Quotation on p. 139 is from "Tomlinson," in *Rudyard Kipling's Verse: Definitive Edition,* and is reprinted by permission of Doubleday & Company, Inc. Quotation on p. 140 from "The Hollow Men" by T. S. Eliot is from *Collected Poems 1909-1962,* and is reprinted by permission of Harcourt, Brace & World, Inc., and Faber & Faber, Ltd. Quotation on p. 143 from *Saint Joan* by George Bernard Shaw is used by permission of The Public Trustee and The Society of Authors. Poem on p. 166, "Verse," by Adelaide Crapsey, is reprinted from *Masterpieces of Religious Verse.*

SET UP, PRINTED, AND BOUND BY
THE PARTHENON PRESS AT NASHVILLE,
TENNESSEE, UNITED STATES OF AMERICA

To———————————

Mrs. May L. Teasley McCurry
and the memory of the late
William Baird McCurry

Men live in crisis. No man alive escapes the crisis situation. It seems to come almost daily. Thomas Carlyle once said, "It was always a serious thing to live!" This is particularly true today. We are up against the bullying forces of nature—just staying alive. The age of progress presents us with crisis and decision. Every day decisions have to be made. What we do in the crisis time determines whether we truly live or slowly die, grow or atrophy, mature or regress into childhood. There is life significance in every crisis.

The dictionary defines a crisis as the crucial moment, the decisive time, the turning point. How many of these there are in life!

There is something more. God is involved in every crisis, in every decision. Carl Michalson wrote in his book *Faith for Personal Crises:* "No crucial situation is adequately lived through . . . which does not take into consideration the dimension of the God-relation. 'What does God intend?' 'What, therefore, must I do?'

These two questions interpenetrate in every crucial situation."

Here is the purpose in these twelve sermons: to recognize that crisis times are common to all mankind; to ask what God intends; and to answer the question, "What can I do?"

My sincere appreciation to Mrs. Helen Colley for preparing the manuscript for this book.

CONTENTS

"Take therefore no thought for the morrow."   —Matt. 6:34

When the Soul Is Cracked
~~~~~~~~~~~~~~~~~~~~~~~Across with Care

One night recently I woke up about one o'clock and got to thinking about some problems that I face, and about all the things I have to do in the near future. Problems of church administration to handle, speaking engagements to fill, papers to write, people to see in hospitals and at home, money to raise. Soon I was very restless, giving the pillow a real workout. Then I decided I'd try something I had been telling other people to do. So I began to say some of the passages out of the Bible that shed light on the matter of worry:

Take therefore no thought for the morrow: for the morrow shall take thought for the things of itself. Sufficient unto the day is the evil thereof. (Matt. 6:34.)

Lo, I am with you alway, even unto the end of the world. (Matt. 28:20.)

The Lord is my shepherd; I shall not want. (Ps. 23:1.)

In all thy ways acknowledge him, and he shall direct thy paths. (Prov. 3:6.)

Trust in the Lord with all thine heart; and lean not unto thine own understanding. (Prov. 3:5.)

I was soon sound asleep again!

These are real promises—not just words. They have solid value for harassed, anxious, worried people. In fact, Jesus preached his greatest sermon to the world's greatest worriers. The people who heard him when he gave the Sermon on the Mount concerned themselves with countless washings, keeping minute laws, fasts, and feasts. They were concerned with their standing among the people, the future, government, taxes, death, economic matters. In fact, the list of their anxieties sounds fearfully like the list of ours. And Jesus said to them, "Do not be anxious!" He says it still today to people who are anxious and fretted and overly concerned with matters that do not really matter. Matthew 6:25-34 suggests an answer to the problem. Men get their minds so set on things around them that they fail to see God. This passage requires a joyous trust in him. "If God so clothe the grass of the field . . . ," implying that he will take care of his human creations too.

Many of us are chronic worriers. Of all the things that destroy spiritual, moral, and physical vitality, none does it quicker than a fretful, anxious attitude toward life. Here is something that gets to us all, and no door seems able to secure us against it! In Goethe's *Faust* four gray sisters appear at midnight at the palace door. They are Want, Necessity, Guilt, and Care. The first three cannot get in, but the keyhole is large enough for the entrance of Care, or Worry. And when Faust talked with Care, she replied,

> Though no ear should choose to hear me,
> Yet the shrinking heart must fear me;
> Though transformed to mortal eyes,
> Grimmest powers I exercise.
> On the land or ocean yonder,
> I a dread companion wander,
> Always found but never sought!

Look at our average day. We leap out of bed fifteen minutes later than we should, gulp our coffee, bolt our food, whiz into town, dash for the office, rattle off letters, rush to lunch, tear out home, drop dead! How often do we say, "I'm so frustrated! I'm so worried!" We feel we'd like to resign from the human race, not because life is dull, but because life is too full of so many things—many things we vaguely suspect are not worth our attention and energy. The sin of our lives, at least for most of us, is not idleness but being too busy. We bring most of our anxiety on ourselves by trying to do things that don't amount to anything, then we are frustrated because we didn't accomplish anything. A man made a speech. When he was finished, he kept

13

asking, "Did I do it good?" Finally he asked one man, "Did I do it good?" and the man replied, "You did it good, but it wasn't worth doing!" Some things we must do. Some things others talk us into doing. Some we want to do. It all adds up to more than we are able to do, and pressure from without and frustration from within rob us of power and poise. Overdoing and over-fretting are sins of the worst sort. Nuclear physics has given us a new word: implosion. In personal terms this means the chafing of the personality because of its lack of unity. We often implode before we explode. This is why faith is so important in handling anxiety. Faith gets at the inner causes of anxiety and not just the exterior expressions of it.

Look at some of the things that cause us anxiety and worry: how to pay bills, what may happen in the future, new developments in science and the frightening possibility of the destruction of mankind, fear of death, the realization that we have done wrong, wrong choices, whether the children will turn out well, health, an appointment that must be kept, fear of failure, concern over what people think or say, social standings, encroaching age. Then there are those who just worry. If they suddenly discover that they have nothing to worry about, that worries them. Make your own list, lest I suggest some you hadn't thought of—and give you something else to worry over.

Peter Marshall preached in Washington once on the topic, "The Problem of Falling Rocks." All of us have seen signs in the mountains, "Beware of Falling Rocks."

14

This is a hazard of driving in the mountains. Rate of speed has nothing to do with it; the way you handle your car has nothing to do with it; the condition of the tires makes no difference. The hazard is there. Suppose you decide to drive on and risk the falling rocks. How do you do it? Do you creep along, peering anxiously upward at every rock, stopping to ponder every overhanging rock on the mountainside, wondering if this is the rock that is the hazard? What good would it do to worry about the rocks? Dr. Marshall concludes by saying, "The worrying of the driver has no effect upon the rock, but it has a tremendous effect on the driver." If you go to the mountains, enjoy them, take necessary precautions, drive carefully, but don't worry about the problem of falling rocks. Your vacation will be ruined. So with life. The hazards are there. All of us know that. But the Christian is the one who has learned to trust God, do his best, and leave the outcome in God's hands. Dr. Marshall says: "A good deal of the strain and tension of modern life is due to our unwillingness to accept situations that are beyond our control. Christians must be realists as well as idealists, and Christ was both."

Take a close look at the things that fret you. Do they really happen? The newspaper *The Boston Transcript* used to carry these words on the masthead: "I am an old man. I have worried a great deal about many things, most of which never happened!" John Watson wrote in *The Houston Times:* "What does your anxiety do? It does not empty tomorrow of its sorrow; it only empties today of its strength. It does not make you escape the devil. It only makes you unfit to cope with him when he comes."

Wise Plato wrote centuries ago, "Nothing in the affairs of men is worthy of great anxiety." Another has said that worry is like a rocking chair; it gives you something to do but doesn't get you anywhere. Thomas Carlyle once built a soundproof room in his home in London, so he could do his work without interference from outside noises. His neighbor had a rooster that crowed several times every day and night. Carlyle protested to the neighbor, and the man said that his rooster crowed only three times, and surely that was not a great annoyance. "But," Carlyle said to him, "if you only knew what I suffer waiting for that rooster to crow!" So with us. We wait anxiously for something to happen, sure that it will any minute, and so deplete our energies and dissipate our strength.

Take a careful look at what anxieties do to us. An executive in a large manufacturing company said that four out of five cases of inefficiency were caused by worries about matters outside the business. A young doctor said that 35 percent of the illnesses on his records started with worry. Dr. Charles Mayo said, "I have never known a man who died from overwork, but many who die from doubt." Compare anxiety with cancer. Cancer begins almost unnoticed—some little irritation, something not worthy of our attention. At first there are no signs of it that can be detected. But once it gets hold, it will spread to all parts of the body. So with worry. From an insignificant beginning it grows to tremendous proportions, and may eventually kill us. This is why it is so important that we watch for symptoms and have checkups both for cancer and worry. Anxiety may begin in a simple reaction to a situation. It gets a foothold, crowds out all healthy emotions and responses, and takes over completely. Some wag has written a poem called "The Worry Cow":

> The worry cow
> Would have lived till now
> If she hadn't lost her breath.
> But she thought her hay
> Wouldn't last all day,
> So she mooed herself to death!

Worry can kill just as surely as can cancer. It robs of vitality, poise, the ability to think straight; it makes nervous wrecks of us, takes away radiance of living, makes us mere skeletons of our real selves.

There is a good kind of anxiety, of course. George Eliot said, "It is well that fear should sit as the guardian of the soul, else how should man learn to revere the right?" Carl Michalson said, in *Faith for Personal Crises,* "Nothing significant would ever be accomplished without the aid of anxiety." We must distinguish between thoughtful consideration and useless fretting. Jesus did not encourage careless living by his statement, "Take no thought. . . ." People who make no plans for their lives are often a burden to others. Our home is in a beautiful wooded section of Atlanta. My

17

study is upstairs on the back, looking out on oaks and pecan trees. Often I find myself watching squirrels scamper along the limbs carrying nuts and other bits of food to their nests. They bury things in the ground against cold weather. Jesus said that the birds sow not, nor do they reap, but they make provision for sustaining life. He was not approving careless, unplanned living. He was approving trust in God for everything. Elizabeth Cheney has written:

> Said the Robin to the Sparrow:
> "I should really like to know
> Why these anxious human beings
> Rush about and worry so?"
>
> Said the Sparrow to the Robin:
> "Friend, I think that it must be
> That they have no heavenly Father
> Such as cares for you and me."

Jesus made careful plans for his life. The forty days and nights in the wilderness gave him a pattern. He called his disciples according to a plan. He set up carefully the plans for the Last Supper. He "stedfastly set his face to go to Jerusalem." I am sure his itinerary was planned to give maximum coverage to his message in the few short months he knew he had. There was nothing haphazard about Jesus. Even so, as John S. Bonnell says in *No Escape from Life:* "If Jesus were living in any great city today, He would still say, 'Be not therefore anxious about the morrow!'"

There is vast difference between worry and careful planning. Often careful planning keeps us from worry and anxiety.

The Christian religion has a word to say to those who are anxious, who are fretters and worriers. It seems strange that you find as many fretters among church people—people who are supposed to be Christian and have the answers—as among any other group. Why? Christianity ought to help. The Christian ought to be the most radiant person on earth. He ought to have the answers. What is the matter? The trouble lies in the gap between the religious truths we accept intellectually and the truth we practice in our daily living. It is one thing to sing hymns of trust in church. It is another to live out that trust in the commonplace affairs of every day. Trust does defeat anxiety and worry. That makes us hie to our knees to ask whether we truly trust Christ or just go through some motions. Inner peace comes from learning to manage life where it is and not running away from it. We all face "falling rocks." Our problem is to learn to apply the truths of the Christian faith to practical, everyday, down-to-earth living. The Christian faith has something to say about every area of life, none excluded.

In the first place, we must learn to distinguish between the essential and the nonessential in life. I said earlier that many of the things we do are not necessary or worth doing. Thomas Goodwin, London preacher of the seventeenth century, once said, "If a man should go to London to get a pardon . . . and should . . .

spend his time . . . seeing the lions at the Tower, the tombs in Westminster Abbey . . . or visiting friends, would he not be a fool?" We spend much of our time in nonessential matters. Paul admonished his hearers to "lay aside every weight!" Get rid of hindrances to running. One of the ten requirements for membership in the Coronary Club, is, "Accept all invitations to meetings, banquets, committees." Years ago, I spent some time in a hospital. I got to thinking about all the things I was doing. Many of them were so unimportant that they appeared ridiculous. When I got better I spent several hours dictating letters of resignation from committees and clubs. Look at our social engagements. We give so much time to the trivial that there is little or no time for the important. This is a major difficulty in getting people to work in the church: so much of life is frittered away in clubs and committees and groups that make no worthwhile contribution to life. We major in minors. Many of these things aren't wrong—they just aren't important. "Miscellaneous living" is one of our greatest sins. Decide what matters and get rid of the rest.

In the second place, get rid of the things that cause anxiety. Here are some of them: hatred, self-pity, greed, lust. Buy only what you can pay for. Don't be two-faced. Don't be concerned with praise of the crowd. Don't be afraid to make mistakes or fail. Don't have to hide things from your husband or wife. Don't leave something half done. You see, some common sense will help

20

us rid ourselves of many things that cause anxiety. Get rid of the troublesome things.

Third, live one day at a time. That is all you can do. We are not jugglers. We cannot live in the past or the future. The past is gone, and all we can do about it is seek forgiveness for the mistakes we made. Tomorrow has not come. All we can do is plan wisely and well. But today is here. Live it to the fullest. Dr. Franklin Parker, one of my teachers at Candler School of Theology, loaned me a copy of a book by Sir William Osler entitled *A Way of Life*. It had a single sentence in it that I have not been able to put out of my mind in over twenty years: "If the load of tomorrow be added to that of yesterday and carried today, it will make the strongest falter!" What is past is past. Tomorrow has not come. Why dissipate energy worrying about what has been or what will be? Live now.

It is easy to drive yourself to distraction over what is past. Here is a man anxious over a sin he committed. What can he do? He can get forgiveness for it, forget it completely, and never ever have to worry about it again. Or he can drive himself crazy over it. Think, for example, how many times you will have to tie your shoes in a normal lifetime. If you really think about this, you won't live a normal lifetime! Or you housewives— how many dishes will you wash in the next ten years? And make how many beds? The glory of life is that you have to tie one shoe at a time, wash one dish at a time, make one bed at a time. And every other aspect of life is like that. Live today. Entrust the past and the

21

future to God's mercy and love, and don't worry. Live now.

Thanksgiving is an antidote for worry too. When a man stops to count his blessings, he just can't worry. It would bankrupt the English language for us to try to enumerate our gifts. Take air. This is a blessing from God. We couldn't live without it, and we are not even conscious of its presence! Take water. How much we use it, and how little we appreciate it until we go weeks without any rainfall. Take sunshine. How many blessings we have, and how they keep coming without our effort! And when you stop to count them, you just can't worry. This is part of the wisdom of Jesus. He says in our text, "If God so clothe. . . ." Our blessings are God's doing. He takes care of us in marvelous ways when we trust him. John Oxenham wrote:

> For all things beautiful, and good, and true;
> For things that seemed not good yet turned to good;
> For all the sweet compulsions of Thy will
> That chased, and tried, and wrought us to Thy shape;
> For things unnumbered that we take of right,
> And value first when first they are withheld;
> For light and air; sweet sense of sound and smell;
> For ears to hear the heavenly harmonies;
> For eyes to see the unseen in the seen;
> For vision of the Worker in the work;
> For hearts to apprehend Thee everywhere;—
> We thank Thee, Lord.

And if God does clothe the grass of the field, feed the birds, will he not also watch over us?

22

Consider the value of service to others as an antidote for anxiety. Here again is the meaning hidden in Jesus' word: "If God so clothe. . . ." God is always doing for others. Jesus found his highest happiness in doing for others. None of his actions were for himself. No man ever lived who was so completely outgoing, so completely dedicated to the service of others. "He hath anointed me," quoted Jesus, "to preach the gospel to the poor; he hath sent me to heal the brokenhearted, to preach deliverance to the captives, and recovering of sight to the blind, to set at liberty them that are bruised, to preach the acceptable year of the Lord" (Luke 4:18-19). All for someone else. Kagawa, the Japanese Christian, said, "I read in a book about a man who went about doing good. It disturbs me that I am content with just going about!" George Bernard Shaw described a man as a "self-centered little clod of ailments and grievances, complaining that the world would not devote itself to making him happy." We are here not to get happiness but to give it, not to be served but to serve. John Greenleaf Whittier put it beautifully in "Andrew Rykman's Prayer":

> If there be some weaker one,
> Give me strength to help him on;
> If a blinder soul there be,
> Let me guide him nearer Thee.
> Make my mortal dreams come true
> With the work I fain would do;
> Clothe with life the weak intent,
> Let me be the thing I meant;

> Let me find in Thy employ
> Peace that dearer is than joy;
> Out of self to love be led
> And to heaven acclimated,
> Until all things sweet and good
> Seem my natural habitude.

Unselfish service to others takes our minds off our own problems and needs and gives us respite from anxiety.

Finally, look away from self to God. Fulton Sheen insists that worry is atheism because it is lack of trust in God. The greatest cure for worry is trust in God. When we think of the greatness, the goodness, the adequacy of God, somehow we find our fear-filled minds at rest. Ralph Waldo Emerson suffered a great deal in the loss by death of his little son, Waldo. But in his *Journal* he wrote, "All that I have seen teaches me to trust the Creator for all that I have not seen!" Our two sons, Bill and Charles, have blessed our lives beyond anything that we can ever do for them. I like to watch them at night. After they have had a hard day of play or school, they say their prayers, asking for forgiveness for little wrongs done, asking God to watch over them through the night. Then they sleep. What trust! The heat of the day forgotten. No hate. No grudges. No worries. They trust their parents, and they trust God. And this is the way we ought to live, and, thank God, this is the way we can live. Elizabeth Browning wrote,

> The little cares that fretted me,
> I lost them yesterday, . . .
> Out in the fields with God!

"With God!" That is where we lose all our worries. Jesus could go to the cross because of his perfect confidence in his Father. So may we face all that life can throw at us when we trust him implicitly. Augustine said: "Thou wilt be broken if thou fallest out of thy Maker's hands." Trust God. Do your best. Have no anxiety about anything. Every major threat to us as persons, to abundant life, is overcome in God.

One of my favorite plays is *Green Pastures.* In a moving scene the leadership of the Children of Israel was taken from Moses and given to Joshua. When Moses was asked why he was being treated that way, he replied, "De Lawd's got His plans fo' me." So he watched the Hebrews go on their way to the Promised Land. Then God stepped out from behind a rock and put his hand on Moses' shoulder. Moses knew that hand well. He had felt it before. So he said, "You's with me, ain't you, Lawd?" And God replied, "Co'se I is." And he is with us every one, every day, when our lives are surrendered to him.

"I acknowledged my sin unto thee. . . . Thou art my hiding place."
—Ps. 32:5, 7

Oh, How Could I Have Ever
~~~~~~~~~~~~~~~~~~~~~~~~~~~~~~~~Done That?

A well-known preacher was always taking his temperature to see what his state of health was. One day he got the barometer by mistake. When he read it, it said, "Dry and windy." We are always taking polls, having examinations, taking the temperature of the times to see what is wrong. Much of the time we miss the thing that is really wrong.

Modern man assumes that the word "sin" has no vital meaning for our age; it is as outdated as the Model T Ford. Its meaning has been reduced to trivial mistakes of the flesh. Some time ago, after having preached on sin, I was talking with a woman. She said, "The sermon today didn't apply to me. I'm too old to sin!" I am afraid even to guess at what she had in mind. A poet wrote:

OH, HOW COULD I HAVE EVER DONE THAT?

I don't smoke, I don't chew,
I don't go with boys who do!

As if to say sin is a matter of a few bad deeds.

Modern man insists that sin is an outmoded religious concept, or that it is a matter of cultural conditioning, or that it is a relative matter, dependent upon the attitude of the individual or the situation at the moment. Sin is to others a fiction, a favorite gimmick of the parson to hold timid people in line. It is a skin rash, not to be considered seriously. But oddly enough, the skin rash does not seem to go away. A man went to the doctor with a breaking out on his hand. The doctor was puzzled. He couldn't decide what it was. Finally, he excused himself and went for his medical books. He pored over them, and came back to the man and said, "Have you ever had this before?" "Certainly," replied the man. 'Well, my friend, you've got it again!" said the doctor. And that is the fact about sin.

Others say that sin is something that happened to Adam and Eve, and does not apply to us. But sin is a very real problem, whether we recognize it as such or not. Paul Tournier, in his book *Guilt and Grace,* reminds us of something most of us know from experience: "A guilty conscience is the seasoning of our daily life." Sin is no theological fiction, but a very real friction from which comes all our other difficulties. Tournier said in another of his books, *The Whole Person in a Broken World:* "Modern man struggles in secret with his feeling of guilt. And there lies the true cause of the conflicts

27

that rend society." Another prominent psychiatrist went so far as to say, "Most of the cases of mental derangement of a functional type are due to a sense of guilt." Much of our uncertainty, insecurity, fear, loneliness, and isolation stems from a sense of guilt. With Paul we cry, "O wretched man that I am!" In the darkness of our bedrooms we feel that something has gone wrong. All our laughter and gaiety cannot hide our true feelings of wrongness. And the more we repress this feeling of guilt, the more injurious it becomes to our spiritual well-being. Josef Gander said, "Every epoch has its own typical malady." Ours is neurosis brought on by an amoral civilization, a materialism, a misplaced humanism, an irresolution, a lack of conviction. These things do not meet the deepest needs of the soul. None of us can deny the feeling that something has gone wrong in life. The two things I hear most in counseling are: "Life just doesn't seem to have meaning for me," and "How could I have ever done that?" Life cannot have meaning while we are in a state of separation from God. Without God in our lives there is a sense of unworthiness. Here is the crisis of guilt. We set up an image of ourselves, and we simply cannot live up to it. "Oh, how could *I* have ever done that?"

That brings me to the central question: What is sin? We like to blame our troubles on outside factors: microbes, our wives, working conditions, heredity, the government. A surprising number of people in the United States don't like their looks. There are about two thousand plastic surgeons who remake faces. A

28

friend of mine who is a plastic surgeon said that a lot of people don't like the remodeling job when it is done. They are like a woman who went with her husband for his annual checkup. When the doctor had finished, he said, "Madam, I don't like the looks of your husband." She replied, "I don't either, but he's good to the children!" People blame their troubles on a wide variety of things, but if we could solve the inner problems of our lives, we could face microbes, our looks, our wives, our husbands, even the government. Psalm 32 points out that sin is a matter between a man and God. This is what makes it serious business. God is sovereign of all that is. Our sense of sin comes from our knowledge of God. Guilt is the strain between what we are and what God is. It is the strain between the image we have set for ourselves, based on what we feel about God, and what we actually do. Listen to Adam as he speaks to Eve in *Back to Methuselah:* "It is the horror of having to be with myself forever. I like you; but I do not like myself. I want to be different; to be better; to begin again and again; to shed myself as a snake sheds its skin. . . . That is what makes me sit brooding and silent and hateful." Sin is not a skin rash. It is blood poisoning. We deal too often with symptoms and leave the illness untouched.

What is sin? It is rebellion against God. It is not breaking a code of laws. It is not just breaking the Ten Commandments. It is not so much what we have done but what we are that makes it possible for us to do what we do. What we do is a revelation of what we are. Sin is denial of God. Sin is pride which puts us in the center of the stage where only God belongs. Joseph Parker defined sin as "the raised hand, the clenched fist, the blow in the face of God." It is disobedience, irresponsibility toward him who is life. W. H. Auden talks of "the distance of God." We know what he means, and we know also that that distance is our doing and not God's. Erich Fromm, an eminent psychologist, calls us "inveterate idolators." We worship self. We boast our adequacy to handle life. We turn our backs on God and walk away. An actor in a play on the New York stage said it for us. "Get out, God, we don't need you any longer!" And so we march defiantly up and down life's stage, but afraid, insecure, with meaninglessness gnawing at our vitals, never really knowing what life is about.

A girl had broken up with her boy friend. She sobbed, "It's not what he did; it's just that he never once thought of me!" That is the meaning of sin. We absolutize ourselves, and never once think of God. A little boy was assigned the task of writing a paper on King David. He began, "David was a good and rich king. If there was anything wrong with him, it was a slight tendency to adultery." Sin is more than a slight tendency to anything. It is open rebellion. David put it bluntly in Psalm 51: "Against thee, thee only, have I sinned." David's real sin was not adultery. This was a symptom. His real sin was rebellion against God, putting himself at the center, seeking to serve his own desires without a thought for what God wanted of him.

30

There is but one sin in the final analysis: rebellion against God. The forms of sin may be many, but the substance is old, as old as the human race. It is always one and the same.

Open your newspaper and see the various forms. The lying ad of a loan company says you can find happiness if you get rid of all your bills by borrowing from "us" at an unspecified rate. Happiness is things! Statistics remind us that about 650 people died on our highways Labor Day weekend. They go down as victims of accidents. Many were deliberate in that people drank whiskey before they drove, then played the fool. Others played the fool without drinking. Claude Pittman of Cartersville, once a candidate for governor of Georgia, tells of a woman in Cartersville who could never drive without hitting something or someone. She'd manage to back into somebody every time she came out of a parking place. One day he was driving downtown, and she backed out of a parking place right into him. She got out of the car and apologized profusely, saying it was her fault and that she'd pay. Mr. Pittman heard her out, then said, "Madam, it was my fault." "Your fault?" she asked. "How do you mean?" "Well," he replied, "I was at home a while ago, and I saw you pass on your way to town, and I came on anyway!" Far too many accidents are the result of our rebellion against God, and any other authority.

Read of the murders in the paper. Or the cases of rape. Or stories of young people in trouble. Or study the pictures of war. Or those of race riots. Or, when you

31

get in your own bedroom and turn out the lights, look deep into your own soul and see the hatred and grudges and jealousy and suspicion, the good deeds left undone, the time wasted. These are all symptoms of something else: rebellion against God. Genesis is barely six chapters old when God talks of man's rebellion, and says he is sorry he ever made him (Gen. 6:7). This is the reality of sin. Rebellion against God wastes the very fiber of men's souls. It casts a dark shadow everywhere. It destroys personality. It imprisons the mind. It damns the soul. The Bible is full of it. Modern life is full of it too. T. S. Eliot summed it up in *The Cocktail Party* when he said,

> It's not the feeling of anything I've ever *done*,
> Which I might get away from, or anything in me
> I could get rid of—but of emptiness, of failure
> Towards someone, or something, outside of myself;
> And I feel I must . . . *atone*—is that the word?

Man can stand only so much. After a while these symptoms of sin catch up with him. His insecurity, his fears, his sense of emptiness make him do a lot of things to find satisfaction and peace. The newspaper told recently of a bus driver in New York who ran the same route every day: down the avenue, crosstown, up the avenue, back cross town to the garage, day in and out. One day he could stand it no longer. He went down the avenue, and down the avenue, and kept going—to Florida. He was revolting against all the meaningless-ness of the same old rut every day. And so man revolts against all the things that happen to him because of his rebellion against God. Here is the real crisis of guilt: the strain between what God is, what we see ourselves to be, and what we really are.

But, thank God, this isn't all. Somerset Maugham wrote of Dostoevski, "He is intolerant, arrogant, selfish . . . but that is not the whole story." There is another side to this story. No man is wholly lost to God. The divine image may be broken, the relationship severed. It can never be destroyed. There is a pathetic longing for good, for meaning, in every man's life, a reaching out for the Eternal in the worst of us. But there is something better than our reaching out. God in his love seeks us! It is encouraging to a lost man to believe that a search party is looking for him. This is precisely what Paul meant when he wrote, "But God commendeth his love toward us, in that, while we were yet sinners, Christ died for us" (Rom. 5:8). This is the meaning of Jesus.

God had spoken through nature, prophet, teacher. Men had not grasped the idea that God is love. They saw him in thunder and felt his judgment. But Jesus announced his fatherhood, his love, his tenderness also. He taught it in story: a lost coin, a lost sheep, a lost boy. God is the seeking God. But when men didn't respond to his stories, Jesus found another way to demonstrate God's seeking love. He allowed himself to be killed, not on a golden cross between golden candlesticks on a lovely altar, but on a wooden upright between two thieves! Here supremely he showed that God loves even a penitent thief in the throes of death. Here he

33

opened up the heart of God for men to see it bleed for the rebellious, the lost, the lonely, the frightened. Dying, he prayed for the revolting masses: "Father, forgive them; for they know not what they do." God suffered in our behalf. He showed us in Jesus that he wants our friendship, that we can be "whole persons in a broken world," that we can, by the acceptance of his love, live the good life, the whole life, undefeated by our rebellion. God accepts us as we are. Karen Horney, the psychologist, talks of "the tyranny of the should." I should do this, I should do that. There is no hope here. God never said, "You should do this, or you should be that." He said, "Come unto me." The Christian is the one who accepts God's love as a gift. It is never a merit. This is the antidote for guilt.

George A. Buttrick, in *God, Pain, and Evil,* reminds us of a story from the gold rush days in California. Two sailors were rowing an officer from the mainland to the boat at anchor in the bay. They threw the officer overboard and joined the gold rush. They were caught, tried, and sentenced to death. The gallows was set up on shipboard. But before the hanging, the ship's captain thought it would be well to observe the sacrament of the Lord's Supper. They borrowed a Communion service from a San Francisco church. All on board ship were invited, including the two condemned men.

Why the sacrament—in front of a gallows, of all places? Was it because they knew they were all guilty? . . . Was it because they sensed that only Heaven can make reparation, since the gallows could not bring back the murdered man or mend the sorrows of his family? Was it because they realized that the ultimate law is the law of holy love within the nature of God, and that only he can forgive and restore? At any rate they commemorated a Gallows before a gallows. Maybe the Gallows is set from the foundation of the world! Maybe there, before a Gallows, "the problem of pain" [or sin] is pierced with Light.

On the cross, Jesus let us see the seeking God in all his glory and wonder.

How does man take this gift of cleansing from guilt? There must be a sense of responsibility for oneself and for what one is. The person who acts responsibly for himself is on the verge of happiness. This is not simply a preoccupation with past sins. It is a recognition that one has sinned and a recognition that God has made provision by his own action to redeem that sin. It is a recognition that no man, in his own strength, can handle the consequences of sin. Repentance is not a brooding over the past; it is turning to the future. To be penitent is to turn away from a life of sin to a God who accepts man and in so doing sets him free, enabling him to accept himself. It is God who takes away our sense of guilt and frees us from sin. He takes the initiative. Carl Michalson, in *Faith for Personal Crises*, wrote: "The Christian answer to the crisis of guilt is to show that the burden of guilt is unbearable simply because man is not meant to bear it himself. Only Jesus is the sin-bearer. Because of him, there is therefore now no condemnation."

35

There are several possible ways to handle guilt. We may shrug it off and take it lightly. We may punish ourselves unmercifully, or we may make life miserable for other people because of our own wrongdoing. There is another way. No man need go on as he is. Just as sin is rebellion against God, so our salvation is in relation to God.

Reconciliation means restoration to sonship. Jesus told a marvelous story about a rebellious boy. He chafed under the disciplines of home. So taking his belongings, he went away to "a far country." Now a far country is not necessarily geographical. The boy deliberately separated himself from his father's love. He came to himself, feeling guilty and unworthy over his rebellion. He came home, expecting to pay the full penalty of his wrong. He discovered something he had not really known before: the forgiving quality of a father's love. The father restored him to his place as a son, and gave him a ring, shoes, a robe, and a fatted calf—symbols of restoration! The father treated his son as if he had not sinned. The father accepted him and thus enabled the boy to accept himself. So the crisis of guilt passed. Like the father in the story is our Father. When we come to him in penitence—let the Bible say it: "If we confess our sins, he is faithful and just to forgive us our sins, and to cleanse us from all unrighteousness" (I John 1:9).

Here is why, in the Christian faith, we talk so much of surrender to God. We allow God to do in us what only God can do. This surrender is like the surrender of the light bulb to the dynamo for power, the flower to the sun for beauty, the mind of the student to the process of education for learning. Something happens to the total life of a man when he puts himself in right relationship with the God whom Jesus revealed so clearly. Our deliverance from guilt depends, not upon our worthiness, but upon God's mercy. We receive that mercy when we, by faith that is surrender, accept the love of God for us. The burden of guilt is lifted; we are restored to sonship. Life becomes for us a creative adventure, unmarred by a gnawing sense of wrongness and alienation. We begin truly to live as free men. What a joy! And it is available to all men.

"And straightway the father of the child cried out, and said with tears, Lord, I believe; help thou mine unbelief."

—MARK 9:24

～A Cry in the Dark — and an Answer

One day Jesus took Peter, James, and John and went up on a mountain. For the first time they saw him as he really was. It was such a glorious experience that Peter wanted to build "three tabernacles" and stay there. But Jesus reminded them that they must go back to the valley, where there was need. The moments of high inspiration must always be translated into service.

While Jesus was on the mountain, a pathetic incident took place in the valley below. A man brought his son to the disciples for healing. The boy had been sick a long time, but the disciples could not heal him. Then Jesus came, and the man brought his son to him. But let Mark tell the story: "Master, I have brought unto thee my son, which hath a dumb spirit; and wheresoever he taketh him, he teareth him: and he foameth, and gnasheth with his teeth, and pineth away: and I spake to thy disciples that they should cast him out; and they could not."

Jesus said to his disciples and all standing by: "O faithless generation, how long shall I be with you? how long shall I suffer you? bring him unto me." They brought the child to Jesus, and he asked the father some simple questions. Then the father said, "But if thou canst do any thing have compassion on us, and help us." Jesus made one of his greatest statements: "If thou canst believe, all things are possible to him that believeth." Then the anxious father replied, "Lord, I believe; help thou my unbelief."

All of us know exactly what the man in Mark's story was talking about. "Lord, I believe; help thou my unbelief." That is, we believe some, and in some things. Doubt is a common commodity.

I have been a pastor long enough to be aware of the disturbing doubts, questions, skepticisms that people have about religion. Standing, looking over the average congregation, I am impressed by the calm, reverent, receptive attitude. They sing heartily. They enter into the service with a healthy vigor. Yet I know some are saying that God is dead. Or that God isn't necessary in an enlightened world like ours. Or if there is a God, why all the chaos, pain, suffering? Or if there is a God, why has he allowed men to come to the place where all life can be exterminated in twelve minutes? Or if there is a God, and if he is all powerful, why doesn't he intervene in some of the problems that confront us—population explosion, hunger, disease, poverty, denial of human rights, mental illness?

Doubt is a crisis. There is more potential for crisis at this point than in any of the other things discussed in this book. The very meaning of life is at stake in religious doubt. Everything in life can be doubted save this belief: God is, and God is love. This is basic. It gives life meaning. When we lose this, we fall apart in anxieties, guilt, loneliness.

Bishop J. W. Sommer, one of the outstanding Protestant leaders in Germany at the end of World War II, said that the great problem in Europe was a lack of faith in anything. Across America we have seen a decline in religious faith that is a transforming power. The number of church members has risen steadily. So what? How much effect does church membership have on our daily lives? One man told me frankly that he left his religion at the church door when he left on Sunday. A young woman summed it up when she said, "God hasn't meant much to us. We ignore him." The final test of faith is action. If we believe, then our lives will be changed; and our beliefs will make a vast difference in things about us.

Some of you will say, "This has nothing to do with me. I've been a believing Christian for years!" And yet, there is more doubt in the realm of religion than we ever dream. Much of it is among people who belong to churches and have belonged for years. Religion is fuzzy and hazy to the average man, something nice to talk about, speculate over, but it seldom moves over into the realm of the practical and powerful.

Not a one of us but understands the character created by Robert Louis Stevenson, Dr. Jekyll and Mr. Hyde. We find ourselves believing and doubting, courageous and afraid, loving and hating, serving and snatching. With so many possibilities for great and good living, we are poverty-stricken spiritually. Although we have full stomachs, our souls shrivel and die. We are giants technologically, but pygmies spiritually. Precocious in science, we are adolescent emotionally. We have learned to cure many of the diseases of mankind, but our deeper illnesses go untouched by medicine. When we begin to talk about anxiety and depression and worry and fear, every man can answer "Present!" Ours has been alternately called "the Aspirin Age," "the Age of Anxiety," "the Age of Speed." It stands as a matter of record that more than ten billion sleeping pills were washed down our gullets last year in an effort to soothe jangled nerves and give us some release from our troubles. Harry Emerson Fosdick has said: "Unbalanced budgets anywhere are deplorable, but in troubled times like these unbalanced budgets inside human souls are an especially grave calamity. Many persons today are spiritually insolvent. Life demands from them more than their resources can supply. Like exhausted reservoirs in a drought, whose constant expenditure is unbalanced by adequate replenishment, they run dry."

At the root of the whole matter is religious doubt, a lack of faith in something beyond and above ourselves.

41

Life just must have something to fasten to outside itself. Shakespeare wrote:

> Our doubts are traitors,
> And make us lose the good we oft might win
> By fearing to attempt.

Doubt and skepticism are chilling and degrading. God only knows how many there are so overwhelmed with failure that they doubt themselves and God and everything else. This skepticism has got hold on people all over the world. We say it would take a miracle to change things. Well, miracles are God's business, and that is exactly what I am hoping will happen in some hearts.

Let me hasten to add that not all doubt is bad. There is a lot in our world that ought to be doubted. Communism, for instance. The hellish idea that a white man is just naturally better than a black one. The foolish philosophy that says we can buy our way through life to happiness. The devilish theory that war is inevitable. The base thought that man is inherently bad and there is nothing we can do about it! All through history men have had their doubts, and doubts have made progress possible. Doubt has been called the father of discovery. In medicine, science, and government, doubt has played an important part in advance. This is true also in religion. Jesus was a doubter. He doubted some of the time-honored ideas held by his contemporaries, and worked his way through to a lively, positive faith. For example, "Ye have heard that it hath been said, An eye for an eye, and a tooth for a tooth; But I say unto you . . . , love your enemies." Jesus reached his vital faith by his daring doubts. We have arrived at our present belief that God is love because some men doubted other ideas of God.

We believe in the dignity of man because some men doubted that men were just animals. Life would be tragic indeed if there were no doubts. Take a little boy, for instance. Nearly all little boys think girls are a nuisance, and that God didn't know what he was about when he made them. What a pain to have to sit by one in school! And invite one to a birthday party! Heaven forbid! But there comes a day when a little boy begins to doubt his earlier conviction. Something clicks inside him. He reaches for the comb, hair tonic, and shoe polish. His whole concept of girls is brought into question. And doubt leads to a new family! Mark Twain was once asked what the people of earth would be like without women. He replied, "They would be scarce, mighty scarce!"

Strong faith often comes up out of doubt. Many a man has started his journey to a lively faith from doubt. Some men take their faith over from ancestors like secondhand clothes. This faith is not theirs, but their ancestors'. Vital faith is reached through struggle with doubt. Take Jesus. Even in the last minutes of his life, he was still questing for truth and for solid ground. He cried out, "My God, my God, why hast thou forsaken me?" But his last words betray the fact that he found what he was seeking: "Father, into thy hands I commend my spirit."

Don't feel badly about your doubt, unless you are content to live in it. Be honest about it. So you have doubts. Accept the fact. Get over the idea that to be Christian you have to believe everything in the book. Nor do you have to live always at the same level of faith. There are ups and downs in faith, in emotional life, in temperament. Martin Luther said, "Take hold of Christ as a man, if that is all you can do, and one day you will discover you have hold of God." Don't stop struggling. It is no sin to doubt unless you get content with your doubts and stop and begin to live in them. I get concerned with people who have no doubts. It may just mean that they have sealed off their religion and refuse to think. Some aren't bothered by doubts because they don't think much or believe much. Often the noblest faith grows out of the gravest doubts.

Faith brings both a power and a joy which the individual never dreamed possible. Eddie Rickenbacker said to some men in a veteran's hospital, men who had been badly wounded physically or emotionally, "If there is any one of you who has not yet had an experience of God, my advice to him is to go out after it and get it." This man knows what he is talking about from experience.

Faith is our native breath. We are made to trust. People are always asking, "Where do we get faith?" We have it already. We are born with the capacity for it. We may place it in wrong things, or stifle it, but we have it. Our problem is to put it in the right thing, then encourage and develop it. Doubt defeats and destroys. Faith lifts up and frees. Faith is an essential ingredient in life. It is a requirement. Religious faith is essential to make life complete and satisfying. We have life on our hands. Religious faith gives explanation of ultimate facts—where we come from, why we are here, where we are going.

How do you work through doubt to certainty? How do you develop a religious faith that is vital? The man in the story gives us the clue. He confessed his doubt and faced it. He clung to what faith he had. He cast his doubts on God. And that is better than to fling them on your neighbors. Four things are necessary if we are to pass from doubt to certainty in the Christian faith.

First, there is what William James called "the will to believe." Want to believe. God says, in effect, if you want to know, you can know. The very first step is to hunger and thirst after something. This means opening the whole personality to God. It is the surrender that I have talked about so much. George A. Buttrick calls it "a yearning." This is the thing that sent Columbus seeking a new route to India, the Curies searching for radium, Edison seeking the incandescent light bulb. There must be the desire for a strong faith, a yearning to have a power that will overcome all things, including doubt. Without this desire there can be no saving, sustaining faith. This is saying "yes" to God. The will to believe, the yearning, gives opportunity to the divine revelation. For Jesus said, "He that asketh receiveth; he that seeketh findeth; and to him that knocketh, the door shall be opened." Great faith is a gift and must be yearned after. The failure of so many to find God is not that God has hidden himself. It is just that we have not sought, yearned, believed. This is the first step. The man in the story illustrates this. "Lord, I believe." More than all else he wanted to believe.

The second step is come and see! The man in the story took this step. He came to Jesus. This is all that Jesus ever asked men to do. To the first disciples he said, "Come and see." To others he said, "Come, follow me." "If any man will come after me, let him deny himself, and take up his cross, and follow me." These first disciples lived with Jesus. They heard him talk. They listened to him pray. They saw his power. Then one day Peter blurted out for them all, "Thou art the Christ, the Son of the living God."

This is all I am asking you to do. Want to believe. Then spend time with Jesus. Read all you can about him. Many a man has been converted just by reading the gospel story. Invite him into your life. Think about him. Spend time with him. Come and see. Some of us have worked through our doubts and have found a faith that satisfies. We have discovered that Jesus is for us. He knows his way around this old world better than any one of us. He has set us right about things, helped us see that the universe is good and friendly toward us. He has given a word of pardon for the sense of guilt, peace for worry, power for weakness. He is our man. That is why this sermon. I hope some of you can move on up through any doubts you may have until you arrive at a faith that saves and empowers and makes happy. And if you will spend time in his presence, you too will pass from doubt to certainty.

Then step out on your faith. Jesus said, "If any man will do his will, he shall know of the doctrine" (John 7:17). Don't live by doubts. Begin to live by your faith. There comes a time when you must try it for yourself! That time came for the disciples when Jesus went away from them into heaven and they discovered that all he had said was true. Power was given. They could do the miracles he did. The time comes when we must say, "Suppose this is true." Suppose he can forgive my sin, take away my restlessness, give me confidence for anxiety, peace for fear, joy for sadness, love for hate. Just suppose. And we must act on that faith. One Sunday when we got home from church, there was a baby bird in the driveway that had fallen from the nest. We never found the nest, and the mother didn't show up. We tried to keep the bird alive, but to no avail. The time comes when a little bird must look over the rim of the nest into the empty air and say, "Is it possible that this can hold me up?" Some instinct in him, or his mother's bill, sends him out to try it for himself, and what a surprise. It works! He proves that the air not only holds him up, but lifts him to the heavens!

Samuel Shoemaker insists that we act as if we had faith until we get faith. Peter Bohler told John Wesley to preach faith until he had faith, then he would preach faith because he had faith. Faith is an expectancy of soul. It is not just the will to believe; it is action, too. It is a leap, a thrust. This is what the writer of Hebrews is saying: "By faith Abraham . . . went out, not knowing whither he went." By faith Noah built his ark. By faith Moses went down into Egypt. By faith . . . by faith . . . by faith! That phrase rings throughout the Bible. Faith is daring to act. There comes a time when we must step out. I like the story John A. Redhead tells of how G. A. Studdert-Kennedy found his faith. He was alone at night beside the sea. Above him the heavens were black, dotted with millions of stars. The only sound he could hear was the beating of the waves on the shore. He was alone in the darkness. But he said he was aware of a Presence. He felt it was the spirit of the universe moving there in the dark. He said he felt that night as he was to feel later when he lay in no man's land between the trenches on the field of battle and watched a figure coming toward him. He did not know if it was friend or foe. Suppose he asked, "Who goes there?" Would the reply be a bullet, silence, or a good word? So he felt on this night beside the sea. Suppose he asked this spirit of the universe, "Who goes there?" Would he get an answer at all? Or would there be nothing but the crashing of the waves against the cliffs? He took that chance. He cried, "Who goes there?" He got an answer: God!

Last, arrival! All that has gone before prepares us for the arrival, for victory. The will to believe; come and see; stepping out; and now arrival. We discover that all that has been said about faith is true, and it is even more wonderful than we could ever have dreamed.

One of my favorite poets is Alfred, Lord Tennyson. Over many years he had developed the kind of faith that I have been describing. He believed in immortality. Life was nearly over for him, but he had no fear. One day he was thinking of those lines from John Donne,

> Death, be not proud. . . .
>> One short sleep past, we wake eternally,
>> And Death shall be no more: Death, thou shalt die!

Tennyson thought of the narrow strait that separated the Isle of Wight from England. Many times returning home he had seen the beautiful sunset, heard the evening bells, the "moaning of the bar." The end of this life would be like that: a brief crossing in the twilight, the moving tide, the evening star, and home!

> Sunset and evening star,
>> And one clear call for me!
> And may there be no moaning of the bar,
>> When I put out to sea,
>
> But such a tide as moving seems asleep,
>> Too full for sound and foam,
> When that which drew from out the
>> boundless deep
> Turns again home.
>
> Twilight and evening bell,
>> And after that the dark!

> And may there be no sadness of farewell,
>   When I embark;
>
> For though from out our bourne of Time
>   and Place
> The flood may bear me far,
> I hope to see my Pilot face to face
> When I have crossed the bar.

Faith casts out fear. A young lieutenant sat in his prison cell and wrote his parents what was to be his last letter. He was one of the Doolittle fliers, condemned to death. In the last hours he thought of his girl back home, and of his parents, and he knew he would not see them again in this life. So he wrote: "Don't let this get you down. Just remember that God will make everything right and that I'll see you all again in the hereafter. My faith in God is complete, so I am unafraid!" And when we pass from doubt to the certainty of the Christian faith, we are not afraid of anything, life or death, for we can do all things through Christ who strengthens us!

Some time ago I went to the hospital to see a woman, at the suggestion of her doctor. He insisted that every test showed no signs of organic disorders. He felt that something in her conscience was making her sick. We talked a while. Years ago she had been in love with a man, and she thought they would marry. So they had sexual relations. After a few months he announced that they would not get married. She was brokenhearted.

She subsequently met and fell in love with another man, and married him. They had three lovely children. But this incident before her marriage haunted her. She lived in terror that her husband would find out. Deep down she harbored a love for that first man. She was sick from an overdose of guilt. I asked if she really wanted to be well. She replied that she did and I believed her, so earnest was she. I told her about a little verse in the New Testament: "If we confess our sins, he is faithful and just to forgive us our sins, and to cleanse us from all unrighteousness" (I John 1:9). Then I talked about the way Jesus forgave even those who crucified him. I talked about forgetting the past, putting the man out of her mind. And I asked that she venture out by what faith she had on these promises from the Bible. She took the step. I could see victory written all over her face. When the doctor came the next day, she told him she didn't need to be in the hospital, and he dismissed her. She was well. This is the curing power of just a little faith.

Or, here is a young couple. When they married a few years ago, they were very much in love. But along the way they began drinking and going with a fast crowd, spending time in bars and nightclubs and rarely going to church, though both of them grew up in the church and for years were active in it. Gradually they began to drift apart, and got interested in other people, until one day they woke up to the fact that they were in a lawyer's office talking about a divorce. Divorce? Us? It couldn't be. That is when I saw them again. I had married them and had told them that if they ever got into trouble, to please call me, and give me a chance before going to see an attorney. We talked, and I could see remorse and guilt all over them. Without asking, I knew they wanted to get things right. Then they told me so. I could see that their hands were already clasped. So once again, as I had done years before, I told them the meaning of marriage and its beauty and sacredness. I asked if they really wanted to make it work, and if they believed they could. Both questions received an affirmative answer. Then let's take the venture. Let's try it. We went to the sanctuary. I performed the wedding again, and we knelt at the altar. I suggested ways by which they could develop their faith and make their home happy. Today they live in another city. They are radiantly happy, and both are vitally at work in the church. Faith works wonders.

You can pass from doubt to the kind of certainty Paul was talking about when he said, "I know whom I have believed, and am persuaded that he is able to keep that which I have committed unto him against that day" (II Tim. 1:12). You don't have to go on in your doubts, defeated and frustrated. Robert Herrick wrote:

> Lord, I am like to mistletoe,
> Which has no root and cannot grow
> Or prosper, but by that same tree
> It clings about: so I by thee.
> What need I then to fear at all

So long as I about thee crawl?
But if that tree should fall and die,
Tumble shall heaven, and so down will I.

God is alive, and when our faith in him is vital and strong, then we are alive too.

"Let every man, wherein he is called, therein abide with God."
—I Cor. 7:24

Shall I Ever Be Asked For? Am I
~~~~~~~~~~~~~~~~~~~~~~~~~~~~~~~Wanted? Needed?

"I hate it! I hate it! I hate it! Every morning, five days a week, I catch the 7:25 bus, stand up to town, face the same people, answer the same telephone, reply to the same stupid questions. And all for what?" Or listen to this: "I was educated for a profession. Deep down, of course, I wanted to be a housewife and a mother. I married. Now there are children. I am bored with dishes and diapers and screaming children to the point of climbing the wall. And my husband thinks I have nothing to do but eat chocolates and read comics all day." Outbursts like these about work are more common than we know.

One fourth of our time, or more, week after week

is spent in the work arena. How often does the question arise, "Am I wanted? Needed?" In *The Age of Anxiety,* W. H. Auden speaks of the crisis in the soul of the young, trying to decide about work, waiting for a call, looking for a niche. It is crisis, not for youth only, but for all men.

> . . . . To be young means
> To be all on edge, to be held waiting in
> A packed lounge for a Personal Call
> From Long Distance, for the low voice that
> Defines one's future. . . . The fears we know
> Are of not knowing. Will night-fall bring us
> Some awful order—keep a hardware store
> In a small town. . . . Teach science for life to
> Progressive girls—? It is getting late.
> Shall we ever be asked for? Are we simply
> Not wanted at all?

There are few facts that need more urgently to be learned than that your job and mine—the kind most of us do—can be more than punishment for being human. We got that idea from the book of Genesis. After the fall of Adam and Eve, God drove them from the Garden of Eden with the words: "In the sweat of thy face shalt thou eat bread, till thou return unto the ground" (Gen. 3:19). For millions, work has neither dignity nor interest. It is a burden, a necessity to be borne. Life does not begin until work is done. Hosts of people work only so they can stop work. Too many people think of work not as a producer of happiness, but only as something to be endured until enough money is accumulated.

A fellow of twenty-eight made a fortune in stock. He died at the age of eighty-eight recently. He was a nice sort of fellow. He never did any harm—just flitted from one resort to another. He never did any good or creative thing with himself or his money. Yet we insist, "Oh, that I had enough money so I wouldn't have to work!" Contrast that man with a chemistry student, working on a course requiring seven or eight years. A relative died and left him a small fortune. What to do? Live it up? Why not? What would you do? He set up the money in an account to further research and went on to school. You'll hear his name some day. Somewhere he has learned a mighty secret: work is not our mortal enemy. Thomas Carlyle was right: "All true Work is sacred; in all true Work, were it but true hand-labor, there is something of divineness. . . . Sweat of the brow; and up from that to sweat of the brain, sweat of the heart . . . up to that 'Agony of bloody sweat,' which all men call divine."

Work is a necessity, not just to live, but to satisfy some basic emotional needs. Because it is so basic to life, there are crises. Almost all people face a crisis in work soon or late.

There is conflict between what a man can do and what he would like to do. Many a man has the urge to do something he is not qualified for. Carl Michalson quotes a man as saying, "I would rather be a second-rate lawyer than a first-rate clerk." Sometimes we just aren't equipped in any respect to do what we want to do and have to settle for something less, or different, or beneath our ideals.

There is the sheer monotony of some jobs. To stand day after day and put the same kind of screw in the same little place on the same kind of frame, time after time, and never see the finished product, never have contact with producer or owner, creates conflict. To wash the same dishes three times a day, even to face the same typewriter eight hours a day five days a week, pound out two sermons every week—this produces boredom and crisis. During the days of the WPA, men were moving dirt with wheelbarrows. They pushed them ahead of them, emptied the load, and went for another. The boss saw one man dragging his wheelbarrow behind him. He asked him what was the matter. The man said with dejection written all over his face, "I'm tired of seeing the blasted thing!"

Often there is an open clash between service and self-interest. The young person finishing college with a degree in teaching must face a choice. Shall I teach in the country, where teachers are hard to get, good ones are needed, and the work is hard; or shall I teach in the city where the bright lights are? The doctor faces the same choice. Shall I be a general practitioner, find a place where no doctor is, and serve needy people; or shall I specialize and serve only the silk-stocking trade? If I were going to be a doctor, I think I'd be a dermatologist —a skin doctor. Nobody ever dies of skin problems, and nobody ever really gets well.

Sometimes the job itself involves moral values too. For example, a young man was offered a promotion. He knew that if he moved into the executive branch of his company, he would be required to do some things against his conscience. He would have to take customers out to questionable places, buy them drinks, give whiskey at Christmas. He would have to stretch the truth. He knew that in his company expense accounts were padded. What to do? Should he compromise and salve his conscience by saying his family needed the extra money, or turn it down and be true to his convictions? Or, here is a man on the assembly line. He admitted that he slowed down production to make the job last longer. Or another put inferior materials in a building to increase his profit. These decisions about work produce tension.

To need appreciation in work and not get it may create a crisis too. A young woman told about her boss. "He doesn't care how I do the work. He doesn't care if I live or die. Just get it out. Never a kind word of encouragement, never a word of thanks!" So what incentive is there to do well and improve the job? Two men were talking at the office one day about their wives. "Do you ever take your wife gifts when you go home at night?" one asked the other. "Never have," replied his friend. "Well, you ought to try it. It would make her appreciate you and love you more." That afternoon on the way home, the man thought about it. He'd never taken his wife anything. So he stopped and bought her a dozen red roses; at the drugstore he got a box of candy; at the bookstore he got a book and several magazines; and at the department store he bought her a bottle of perfume. When he got home, she met him at the door. He handed her the gifts. She looked at them for a moment, then began to cry. "What's the matter with you?" he asked. "Here I bring you all these nice presents, and you stand there crying like a baby!" "This has been the worst day I ever lived," his wife said. "This morning about ten o'clock the water heater burst. At noon the cook got mad and quit, and now you come home drunk!" Appreciation, given so seldom, may come as a surprise. But try it with those with whom you work. It works wonders.

Sometimes a young man comes into a business and right away gets a promotion over several men who have seniority. Each of the older men thinks, "I should have had that promotion. I've been here longer, know more about the business. But they bring in this young whippersnapper. . . ."

Automation produces many a crisis situation. Work is considered a universal right. Unemployment strikes a deadly blow at a man's sense of dignity and worth as a human. His being is at stake. Here is his one opportunity to prove his worth. Then the machine is hauled in, and he hears, "We don't need you any longer." To face unemployment creates an emotional crisis that is dangerously destructive.

Retirement produces crisis too. Many a man comes to compulsory retirement unprepared for it. No matter how he may joke about what he plans to do, the time comes and suddenly he realizes that he is no longer wanted, and will never be called for again. A woman described her husband's retirement this way: "Twice as much husband and half as much pay." The question after retirement is: How shall I keep creative without my job?

And youth face the crisis of choice. What shall I do with my life. Shall I seek the job that pays the most money, regardless of what it is; or shall I look for something that will serve man and help me grow, something that will use all my powers, allow me to be creative, and make me a better person?

You see, in the area that takes one fourth or more of our time, there is the possibility of grave crisis. How is crisis dispelled? It is dispelled by getting a new attitude toward work. We have forgotten something. We might say that the Christian's word for salvation is "vocation." In the New Testament vocation was God's call to man—a call which delivers man from sin, the devil, and death. The Christian has one vocation. God calls every man to the same vocation: to be a holy, godly man, to become God's child, to become a member of the body of Christ, to forsake everything that would keep him from being his best, to be filled with the Holy Spirit. Different people choose different jobs, different professions. God gives men different gifts. Some can paint, some can sing, some can speak, some work with their hands, some handle money, some teach. Some are plumbers, some barbers, some secretaries. These are professions by which we earn money to sustain us while we carry out our true vocation; that is, to glorify God, to enjoy him and serve him. God calls every man to one vocation: to be thoroughly Christian, forsake sin, and live the good life in every area of activity.

In dealing with people, I find quite a few who say they hate their jobs. They don't really hate their jobs, they hate themselves. I was in a plant a few days ago. It was so clean you could almost eat on the floor. The manager showed me through. Machinery did the work hands once did, and the backbreaking drudgery had been removed. But the manager pointed out with pride that automation did not deprive even one of his men of work. Then he startled me with his next statement: 'We are letting the universe work for us. We have harnessed new powers." He was talking about machines. I stood there thinking about men. Long ago it was said of Jesus Christ, "But as many as received him, to them gave he power to become the sons of God." That's the power we need in our jobs. When we hate a job, the trouble may not be in the job but in the man. When our hearts are changed by the power of the Lord, then we can transform our jobs. Our first call is to be Christian— Christian up to the limit of our ability. Then we can handle the job.

Consider another thing. In God's eyes no job is worth more than any other. Helmut Thielicke, in *The Trouble with the Church,* suggests that "there can be no quantitative approaches to salvation by means of merits, by lifting the level of our accomplishments." We have placed too much emphasis on happiness in our work. A job can be pure drudgery and yet produce a satisfaction and joy if well done, and if done for the right reasons. Many are unhappy in their work because of wrong motives; work is simply a way of keeping soul and body together. This was never the motive for work in Jesus' eyes. He placed a halo around work by working in a carpenter shop himself, by doing a good job, using honest materials, giving good measure. This gave him a sympathy for all who use minds or hands in toil. We want the executive places, forgetting that even in the dull, routine jobs we can glorify God and serve our fellowman. It is reported of Brother Lawrence, "He was never hasty nor loitering, but did each thing in its season, with an even, uninterrupted composure and tranquillity of spirit. 'The time of business,' he said, 'does not with me differ from the time of prayer, and in the noise and clatter of my kitchen, while several persons are at the same time calling for different things, I possess God in as great tranquillity as if I were upon my knees at the blessed sacrament.'" Any job can be transformed and made a sacrament.

But there is something else to remember: Our work life is the arena where our faith is finally tested. Worship on Sunday ought to be a launching pad to send us into the week to practice our faith, even in the drudgery of work. The life of faith cannot be suspended during working hours if the life of faith has validity. Numbers of people insist that they cannot be Christian at work and hold their jobs. They must work, for there are family obligations. But rather than make their jobs a testing ground for faith, they make no pretense of being Christian at all. The important thing is for a man to learn to think of his work in a Christian way. The scientist, the radio operator, or the engineer ought to be able to say, "In the work I am doing, I am a partner with God, helping him with his work of creation, and the realization of his purposes for the whole family of mankind." Martin Luther said:

A cobbler, a smith, a peasant, whatever he may be, and man has the labor and occupation of his craft, and yet all men alike are conservative bishops and priests. A poor servant girl may say: "I cook the meals. I make the beds. I dust the rooms. Who has bidden me do it? My master and my mistress have bidden me. Who has given it them? So it is true that I am serving God in heaven as well as them. How happy I can feel now. It is as if I were in heaven doing my work for God."

One of the most hopeful signs in Protestantism is the increasing witness of the laity in everyday tasks. In fact, there are training programs to teach laymen to do this effectively. We talk about the renewal of the church as if it were some hazy something that would float down out of the sky. Renewal in the church will come with renewal in the man in the pulpit, when his preaching takes on meaning, relevance, validity, and with renewal in the man in the pew, so that he carries his religion outside the walls of the sacred place. Whether it be the kitchen or the office, a road grader, or a mill, the work arena is the place where our faith is finally tested.

63

My job as a preacher is no more sacred than yours, whatever you do. My first calling was not to be a preacher. Just like your calling, mine was to be a Christian. My first calling was to salvation. I then felt that God was leading me into the profession of minister of the gospel in the church. I have felt that this is the place where I can best serve God and man with the small gifts I have. But I have a responsibility to make my profession an arena where I can witness to what God's love means to me as a person, and to what happens in the life of a man who heeds God's call to salvation. We have made too much distinction between the work of preacher and of layman. We are both called with the same calling, and each has the same responsibility to make his work a witness to his Lord. Someone described William Gladstone, Prime Minister of Great Britain: "He was a Christian politician, which is sometimes more than being a Christian bishop." And it is, if the politician is more Christian in his politics than the bishop in his affairs.

We must see our work as a service to God and man. In some jobs it is hard to see the service angle. But here is where much of the crisis that arises in work can be dispelled. If we can see ourselves made in the image of God, stewards of his good things, recipients of his mercy and love, accountable to him, responsible for our fellowman—this will give us an enthusiasm for our jobs, no matter what they are. Work is not just intended to bring in money. No man can be happy with just money. It does not touch the deepest needs of a man's being. A friend of mine advertised for a young man to become a part of the business. A lad of twenty-one answered. His first question was, "What kind of retirement system do you have?" Nothing about service! Take away the service aspect of work and you rob it of its deepest meaning.

Seeing our work as a way of serving God introduces an enthusiasm into it. Walter Chrysler used to say, "The only way to meet this life is to get excited about it! Believe in it with all your heart. Get enthusiasm in your soul. Make yourself enthusiastic, practice it, and after a while you will find that you have enthusiasm." If you go to work dragging, then the job will be a job, nothing more. Frank Bettger wrote *How I Raised Myself from Failure to Success in Selling,* attributing his successful career to his real enthusiasm for his job. Love it. See it as a chance to work with God and serve mankind. It may not be the best job, but seeing it in this way will help make it such. An old priest used to say, "It is not only prayer that gives God glory, but work." See your job that way. Go to work tomorrow morning saying, "I'm working at this job to help God make his world a better one for me and for all his children."

Then expect a reward from your work. All work deserves fair pay. Some people get too much pay for too little work. Some get too little pay for too much work. We need money to live. It is not sinful to work for money. But if we work only for money, if this is the only reward we get, then we aren't living up to the full. An old Negro preacher in Charleston used to say that most of his pay was hidden salary. By that he meant the satisfaction of serving man, of seeing lives change, of being a partner with God in the great venture of life. The man who dedicates the day's work to God finds some rewards that satisfy. When Jesus came to the end of his earthly life, short though it had been, he could say, "I have glorified thee on the earth: I have finished the work which thou gavest me to do" (John 17:4). His reward came in faithfulness, in his integrity in following his Father's will, and in his service to man through his work. Jesus asked a great question: "What shall it profit a man, if he shall gain the whole world, and lose his own soul? Or what shall a man give in exchange for his soul?" (Mark 8:36-37). Many a man loses his soul over his work! Great rewards in living aren't in money, for this is about the least valuable thing on earth. The great reward is in being a right person, being Christian on the job, serving God, and using one's abilities to lighten the load of humankind. This is the meaning of our text: "Brethren, let every man, wherein he is called, therein abide with God."

Years ago a sociology class at Johns Hopkins University made a scientific study of one of the worst slum areas of Baltimore. The students went into the homes, noted the good and bad influences in the neighborhood, then tabulated their findings. Two hundred cards were marked "headed for jail." On each card was the name of a boy or girl whose home background, attitude toward life, and prospects seemed to indicate a life of crime ending in jail.

Twenty-five years went by, and another class in sociology found the stack of cards marked "headed for jail." They took as their class project checking out the cards to see what happened. They were in for a surprise, for of the two hundred, only two ever got to jail. There was a reason. That reason was "Aunt Hannah." She was a teacher in the grade school in the slum section of Baltimore. One man told his story and illustrated what Aunt Hannah had done. "I sure was a bad egg. I was the worst kid in the neighborhood, and how the cops did like to pin anything and everything on me. And they were usually right. One day Aunt Hannah kept me after school. She told me I was too smart a kid to be getting into trouble, and before I left, she asked me to come to her home for dinner the next Sunday. I just never had the heart to let Aunt Hannah down after that; and now I'm a doctor in this same community." And when Aunt Hannah was asked about it, all she would say was, "Oh, I just loved them like they were my own boys and girls. I just invested my time and talents and love in two hundred children."

God's call is the same to every man. In his eyes no job is worth more than any other. Our work life is the arena where our faith is finally tested. We must see our work as an opportunity to serve God and man. There are rewards to faithful work.

Go to work tomorrow with these ideas ringing in your mind. Put them into practice, and you will find yourself transformed, and your job will be transformed as well.

"For this cause shall a man leave his father and mother, and shall be joined unto his wife, and they two shall be one flesh."
—Eph. 5:31

Successful Marriage — Always a Triangle

Not all is sweetness and light in marriage. This, the most idealized of all human relationships, is filled with potential for crisis. Marriage is the most delicately balanced of all human relationships. It is filled with possibilities for beauty and wonder and greatness. It is at the same time fraught with possibilities for grave crisis.

Someone is always asking, "Aren't you surprised at the large number of divorces?" Saddened, but not surprised. Surprised that there aren't more, actually. Here are two people, different as human beings can be, different in background, in education, in outlook, in ambition, who all of a sudden begin to live together. Crisis is highly possible. While the number of divorces is alarming, this is not a true barometer of the health of marriage. Many homes stay together in torment rather than risk public opinion, or for the sake of the children, or for other reasons. Then there are millions of homes that are happy.

We poke fun at the institution of marriage, take it lightly, abuse the idea in joke and song. But who would vote to do away with it? A husband and wife were having an argument. It waxed hot. Finally he said, "I can't understand why God made women so beautiful but so dumb!" She replied sweetly, "I can answer that. He made us beautiful so you'd love us, and dumb so we'd love you!"

The form of marriage is on trial for its life. With revolutions everywhere, one of the most amazing is taking place in the family. Carl Michalson, in *Faith for Personal Crises*, reminds us that "the frequency of divorce is transforming the structure of marriage into a polygamous form. To be sure, it is only a 'one-at-a-time polygamy.'" But polygamy nonetheless! Difficulties in marriage have always been great. They are accentuated today by our easy mobility, our lack of community, emerging new codes of morality, a lack of stability, a crass materialism. Crisis comes in all marriages, for marriage exists under tension. Marriage is an almost universal experience. That one does not choose to marry does not do away with the crisis. Dr. Michalson says truly, "Marriage is indicated for the human race universally in the nature of bi-sexuality. Therefore, all

states in life must be defined in relation to marriage."
The questions most frequently asked are, "Are you
married?" "How many children have you?" So every
state is defined in terms of marriage.

There is no more beautiful description of marriage
than that in Paul's Ephesian letter. In the fifth chapter
Paul compares the love of a man and a woman for each
other with the love Christ bore the church. It is to be a
holy love, a sacrificial love, a love that is eternal. And
Paul closes his analogy by saying that for this kind of
love a man should leave his father and mother and be
joined to his wife. A wonderful thing happens. The two
become one flesh.

Since crisis is so common in marriage, let us examine
some of the basic causes.

Selfishness is a chief cause. In counseling for marriage, I spend a great deal of time on this point. After
twenty-two years I am sure that a basic cause of trouble
is the unwillingness of one partner, or both, to share in
the deepest sense. No matter what reason for trouble is
given, this one does not lie far away. Adequate preparation for marriage is essential. People need to examine
their motives. When we marry for security, or because
of an emotional need for love, or for what another can
give us, we are headed for crisis at the start.

Marriage is made up of sharing in all the relationships
of life. Not just in sex, but in time, friends, ambitions,
ideals—little things like movies, music, flowers; great
things like the Christian faith. This is what Paul meant
by "they two shall be one flesh." Sharing in sex is im-

portant, but sexual harmony has been oversold. Sexual harmony never is a guarantee of happiness in marriage. We have undersold spiritual compatibility. We love, not for what one can give us or do for us, but simply because one is. "I love *him* just because he is!" This was the lament of a young wife who suspected that her husband wanted her only for what she would give and not for herself. Christ loves the church just because it is. This is the kind of love we bear each other in marriage. On this kind of love a marriage can become beautiful.

An à la carte attitude toward marriage is a second cause of crisis. "If it doesn't work out, we can get out." So I frequently hear. A young woman of twenty asked that I perform her marriage ceremony. I asked if she had been previously married. "Yes," she replied. "Twice. They didn't work out." David Cohn called this kind of marriage "a temporary agreement, like buying a stove on thirty days' trial."

Divorce laws are strict enough in most places. They should be uniform over the country, and some inequities should be corrected. Our chief problem lies not in divorce laws but in preparation for marriage. We spend more time choosing a china or silver pattern than in getting emotionally, spiritually, physically ready for the experience. We look on marriage as an arrangement that can be changed at whim, rather than as something permanent. Such an attitude makes divorce easy.

Of course, there are situations that can be handled only by divorce. The ideal is no divorce. The church ought to labor toward this goal. But when and if divorce becomes necessary, as it sometimes does in our scheme of things, it ought to be done as a last resort, in sorrow and penitence over failure, and never flippantly or with a festive atmosphere—as I have known to be the case. Marriage is forever, and if more couples began it with that conviction, more marriages would succeed.

We Americans are a funny lot. We think we know all about sex and are surprised to find that much we know is half true, an old wives' tale, or not true at all. A misunderstanding of sex brings many a crisis in marriage. We separate sex from the other aspects of life and treat it as a commodity, a thing, to be used or bartered. You cannot separate man into soul and body. He is tied up in one bundle in life. The church maintains that sex is good, it is sacred. Man perverts sex. It is instituted of God for the propagation of the human race. It is a God-given way to meet some psychological needs that cannot be met otherwise. It is the highest consummation of love between two people. In a sense it is a sacrament. Sex is the supreme language of love. Physical union is the expression of an inward and spiritual grace.

Sex involves person. We have dehumanized it and made it an object. We see people as things and not as persons. When we do, we can use the bodies of others, even those we are supposed to love the most, to satisfy our own needs, without concern for the needs of the other person or what our selfishness may do to that person. This is the danger in the "playboy" movement. Women become sex symbols, not persons, and are exploited in personality, used for physical enjoyment and often for financial gain.

Sex requires social responsibility. This is why the church has insisted on chastity before marriage and faithfulness afterward. The real sickness in the sexual revolution is "love" apart from any marriage responsibility. *Look* magazine carried a report on a survey made among a hundred young adults in the United States on the subject. A student of twenty-two was asked about his night life. Was love the real object? "Love? You must be kidding. Sex. Good old healthy sex is what I want. I don't need love." He distinguished between love and sex this way: "Sex is conquest. Love is surrender. Who wants surrender?" Love is devotion. For the sex relationship to have vital meaning, it requires the continuity, the responsibility, and the fulfillment of marriage. For sex in marriage to be what it ought to be, it must be seen as a complete union between two people —physical, yes, but spiritual and emotional as well. Married love is committed love. The sex act is the realization of full communion between two persons (not things) fully committed to each other in love.

A great many people are disillusioned over the seeming change in the character and quality of love after marriage. Novels and movies show a kind of love that is deep and vital and abiding during days of courtship. Courtship is a brilliant and a scintillating thing. Marriage follows as a consequence. Then each immediately begins to look for somebody else! This is the exact opposite of the truth. Elton Trueblood, in *The Common*

73

Ventures of Life, tells us, "Often the deepest love comes after marriage rather than before and is clearly its consequence." This is not just "often"; it is "always" when two people love each other in the highest sense. We could not stand romantic love forever. The emotional strain would be too great. Married love has a beauty and a wonder all its own. It is more nearly akin to Paul's description of love in I Corinthians 13.

Much of what we call love is physical attraction. Much of it is selfishness: "I love me and want you." This is love in the kindergarten stage. Love that lasts involves all of a person—mind, soul, body, all one is and has. It implies respect and understanding. It desires only the best for its object. It wants to give rather than get. It is an earnest and unbreakable goodwill. There is nothing selfish about it. When romantic love has moved beyond marriage and has deepened into the thing of beauty it should become, it bears the daily load of work, the irritations of child care, the failures and successes of everyday life. It keeps kindly. It rejoices in right and good. The "sweet nothings" whispered in the ear before marriage take on substance and become sweet somethings. Love is spiritual oneness that binds two lives inseparably together in every detail for eternity.

Successful marriage is always a triangle: a man, a woman, and God. One source of crisis in marriage is the divorce of religion from marriage and the family. We treat marriage as a civil ceremony and go to minor law officers for the service. Marriage is ordained of God.

74

It is a spiritual matter, necessarily regulated by the state. To divorce God from it is to invite disaster. Augustine said that if we have fallen out of the Creator's hands, we have broken in pieces. Nowhere is that more nearly true than in marriage. Bishop Hazen G. Werner wrote in *Christian Family Living,* "A Christian marriage is one in which this deep, affectional feeling is constantly renewed at the throne of grace and made certain by the underrunning consciousness of that union as being absolute."

Several years ago I went to visit a new family in our community. They had built a lovely home in a beautiful residential section of the city. A gracious lady answered my knock and invited me in. We sat in the living room and talked awhile. Then she invited me to see the rest of the house. It had everything. Every gadget imaginable had been built in. We went back to the living room, and I told her I had come to talk about the Christian faith and the church. She smiled sweetly and said, "Mr. Myers, we don't need religion. We've got everything we need." No wonder there are crises in marriage.

The Christian faith, held in common by two people in love who have prepared themselves for marriage, gives a platform from which to move to settle disputes and misunderstandings. There is a basis on which to meet other crises—death, sickness, loss of job, the failure of a child, and the multitude of irritations that come daily to a family. I always talk with a couple about their faith and their religious practices prior to marriage. No home can be fully successful without God in it! And no nation can long endure unless its homes are godly, grounded in the faith. Edward R. Gibbon, in *The Decline and Fall of the Roman Empire,* suggests as one reason for the fall of this mighty nation the decay in family morality. God in the home goes far toward insuring happiness in the family, and greatness in the nation as well.

I have mentioned five sources of crisis in marriage. Here, then, are three indispensable ingredients in a happy, successful marriage.

First, marriage must be seen as eternal. Jesus spoke plainly when he said, "What therefore God hath joined together, let not man put asunder" (Matt. 19:6). Louis H. Evans, in *Your Marriage—Duel or Duet,* tells of a North Dakota judge who said to a young couple being divorced: "According to the laws of the State of North Dakota, I must declare you free from the bonds of marriage, but may I remind you that probably on the books of Almighty God you are still husband and wife." That is straight talk indeed, but something that needs saying. We take marriage too lightly. Essential to a happy marriage is the shared conviction that it is forever. You may not have got the best deal. You may think of several people you might have married, but you married this one. Now get to work to make it a great marriage.

A woman wrote the Secretary of Agriculture of the United States and said: "You help farmers with their problems; now I need some help. I have dandelions in

76

my yard. I have mowed them down, dug them up, burned them off, poured chemicals on them, but still they come. What can I do?" The Secretary wrote her back: "Madam, if you have mowed them down, dug them up, burned them off, poured chemicals on them, and still have them, I would suggest that you learn to love them!" Marriage must be seen as eternal.

Second, marriage must be seen as spiritual. Carl Michalson reminds us that "the blood of Christ can be the glue of marriage." Marriage revolves around something. How important it is that it revolve around Someone: God. Take a wheel. Around the outside is the rim. In the center is the hub. The spokes run from rim to hub. The closer the spokes get to the center, the closer they get to each other. So in marriage. The closer two people get to God, the closer they get to each other! On the flyleaf of a prayer book in the chapel at the University of Virginia, I found these words penciled:

> Christ at the marriage altar,
> Christ on the bridal journey;
> Christ when the new home is set up;
> Christ when the baby comes;
> Christ when baby dies;
> Christ in the pinching times;
> Christ in the days of plenty;
> Christ when the wedded pair walk toward
> sunset gates;
> Christ for time;

Christ for eternity;
This is the secret of home.

The anonymous author of that poem knew the secret of a happy marriage. We have worn out the old cliché, "Families that pray together stay together," but nothing has come along quite as expressive of the truth. Marriage must be seen as spiritual.

Third, marriage must be seen as sacrificial. There must be a willingness to give, to bend, to compromise. Here is a mark of maturity: to be able to look at a problem from all sides objectively and reach a conclusion good for *us*. The answer may not be what I want, or what you want, but it is best for us. Marriage involves sacrifice by each partner.

Husband and wife must try to understand each other, even at the sacrifice of pride. Little things are disastrous. Sacrifice is essential in handling "the littles" successfully. Neglect and carelessness are twin threats to marriage. So we go out of the way to remember to be kind, attentive, loving. "Sweet nothings become nothings unless we make an effort. "There's no need to chase the bus after you've already caught it" is a deadening attitude toward the needs of the marriage partner. Lovemaking, even at some sacrifice, is mighty important to happiness in marriage. To be able to communicate is vital and requires some sacrifice in effort. To be perfectly honest is not always easy, but it is necessary. Greatness in marriage does not require great sacrifice, but rather a willingness to sacrifice in the little things of life. Little foxes spoil the vines in marriage. Little courtesies, little kindnesses, little deeds of love make marriage strong and vital. Marriage must be seen as sacrificial.

There are crises in marriage. There always will be. But when two people love each other, see marriage as eternal and spiritual, and are willing to make the necessary sacrifices for it, there are no crises that can destroy that marriage. Illness may come, financial difficulties may plague, temptations may threaten, the road may be rough and rocky in many ways. But when two people in love take God into partnership, determined to make marriage happy, willingly sacrificing to make it so, they can overcome everything. Successful marriage—always a triangle.

Three hundred years ago Jeremy Taylor wrote:

Marriage is a school and exercise of virtue; and though marriage hath cares, yet the single life hath desires, which are more troublesome and more dangerous, and often end in sin; while the cares are but instances of duty and exercises of piety; and therefore, if single life hath more privacy of devotion, yet marriage hath more necessities and more variety of it, and is an exercise of more graces. . . . Here is the proper scene of piety and patience, of the duty of parents, and the charity of relatives; here kindness is spread abroad, and love is united, and made firm as a centre: marriage is the nursery of heaven. . . . It lies under more burdens [than does the single life], but is supported by all the strengths of love and charity, and those burdens are delightful. Marriage is the mother of the world, and preserves kingdoms of the world, and fills cities, and churches, and heaven itself. . . .

Single life makes men in one instance to be like angels, but marriage in very many things makes the chaste pair to be like Christ.

"Jesus Christ the same yesterday, and to-day, and for ever."
— Heb. 13:8

Everything That's Nailed Down Is
~~~~~~~~~~~~~~~~~~~~~~~~~~~~~~~~~Coming Loose!

George Bernard Shaw once commented that he was sure our world was the one to which other planets sent their insane. Edmund Spenser talks of "the ever whirling wheel of change, the which all mortal things doth sway." If that was true in his day, think how much more it is true today. Change is the order of the day. We have here no continuing city, for the bulldozer is everywhere in evidence. In fact, the bulldozer may well have become a symbol of America. The old hymn says, "Change and decay in all around I see." And we do. Where once was beautiful countryside, now there are miniature golf courses and pink plaster flamingos. We scrape the earth clean of trees, fill up rivers, and think

81

we are going places. The poet Shelley said, "Naught may endure but Mutability"—nothing remains but change. In the play *Green Pastures,* there is the assertion that is fact, "An' everything dat's fastened down is comin' loose."

I saw a parable of this. Several years ago we were on vacation at the beach. I watched some children building a city. They had done a masterful job. They had laid out streets, built houses, set in churches, stores, parks, even a lake. They had left nothing out. But they saw something. The tide was coming in, the waves licking closer and closer. They worked feverishly to get their city done. It was done just as the waves began to wash the base of the wall. All of a sudden there was one big wave, and when it subsided, the city was gone. Nothing remained. This seems to be what is happening in our world.

In twenty years after the close of World War II, more than thirty nations, with a total population in excess of 700,000,000, became independent. There has never been anything like it in human history. And the end is not yet.

On August 6, 1945, a bomb was dropped. Bombs had been dropped for years prior to that. But this was different; it was an atom bomb. One writer described it by saying, "An age has been born before our eyes!" The world has not been the same since. Recent papers carried the statement that at least one third of our people would be wiped out almost immediately in the event of an all-out nuclear war. We sit on a powder keg instead of a nail keg, waiting for the end.

The population of America has moved from country to city. Now more than 70 percent of the American people live in cities and towns. And the population of the United States will increase to 275,000,000 in less than twenty years. The world's population is growing at the rate of 40,000,000 every year.

There have been changes in medicine. Much of the medicine of ten years ago is obsolete. The medicine of John Wesley's day is a laughing matter. A man went into a medical clinic for an examination. The receptionist gave him a long, narrow card and told him to take it with him all the way through the clinic. The first doctor examined his head and punched some holes in the card. The second doctor examined his lungs and punched some holes in the card. The third doctor examined his stomach and punched some holes in the card; and so it went, until he had finished seeing all the doctors in the clinic. The card was filled with holes. He took it back to the receptionist. She made some notes from the card for her files and told him he might have it to take home. He took it home. He happened to have an old player piano. He put the card on the piano, and do you know what came out? "Lord, I'm Coming Home."

Transportation has changed. I came home from Birmingham one night recently in twenty minutes. Thirty-seven minutes from Atlanta to Charlotte, an hour and sixteen minutes to Dallas.

In every area of life there have been changes. If grandma were to come again and look in on our homes, she wouldn't believe her eyes. We live differently; we are a different people. High schools don't give courses in basic cooking anymore, but courses in thawing, in can opening. Grandma would be amazed, and maybe a little disappointed too.

We have become a mobile people. Odell Shepherd calls it living with "roots in mid-air." Bruce Catton, in *This Hallowed Ground,* a history of the Civil War, tells of Lee's army approaching Gettysburg: "It was on its own in a strange land, scooping up supplies from the fat Pennsylvania farming country, driven by an inexorable compulsion—lacking a supply line, it must eternally keep moving, because if it did not it would starve, and whenever and wherever it found its enemy it must strike without delay, no matter how the odds might look." This is the way we live. Always on the march, lacking supply lines to anything beyond ourselves, we move, living spiritually, emotionally, mentally off whatever resources we find in a given hour. T. S. Eliot, in one of his "Choruses from the Rock," said, "And now you live dispersed on ribbon roads." The highway may be competing with the community as the location of our lives. Everything changes.

Theology changes. We imagine that because the world changes, God must also change. But God never changes. Our interpretations of him and our understanding of him must change. Our attitude toward religion changes. A people once grounded in the faith is not sure what it believes now.

Morals change. Where once we had some solid guide-lines about right and wrong, now it seems to be "do what comes naturally." A chaplain on the campus of one of our colleges spoke on sex one Sunday. He said, "Sex is fun. . . . There are no laws attached to sex. I repeat, absolutely no laws. There is nothing you ought to do or ought not to do. There are no rules to the game, so to speak." This marks a radical change from the Bible, or from the moral standards of our country of even twenty-five years ago! We are living with what is being called "the new morality."

Death comes. Financial fortunes wane and disappear. The family breaks up. The title of my sermon takes on meaning: Everything nailed down is coming loose!"

One of the most moving things I have read about modern life is Franz Kafka's allegory *The Castle*. He wrote it in 1926, but the truth in it becomes clearer as the years slip by. He tells the story of Mr. K., who comes to a town to be the surveyor for a count living in a great castle. But Mr. K. can never seem to get to the castle. It always moves away when he approaches it. Mr. K. tries to settle in the town and become a citizen and a part of everything. He finds this impossible too. No one will accept him; no one understands him, or even tries. He cannot find a satisfying relationship with any other person. He is separate, alone. This is something of where we are now. We have been released from many of the ties of morality, religion, class, and even race. We have a freedom in many areas that man never dreamed of having. But instead of becoming happier, man feels alone, alienated from God and man. All these changes have brought their troubles and problems. We think we are making progress, and that change and progress are synonymous. We have held to the escalator idea of improvement for so long that we find it hard to turn it loose. "Every day in every way man is getting better and better." That is hard to defend. Changes have brought deep difficulties.

This is what Browning was driving at in "Paracelsus," when he said,

> . . . I detest all change,
> And most a change in aught I loved long since.

Men like ruts. Change disconcerts, upsets, even though we equate change with progress. Change disturbs man's equilibrium. Maybe this is our greatest problem: too many changes, and mostly on the outside.

Jesus never suggested that we try to escape our troubles like a Simeon Stylites by climbing a forty-foot tower in order to avoid evil. There is a desperate need for something or someone beyond self. We cannot find security in change. We find it in him only. Here the Christian faith plays its most important role. Change around us calls for a security within us. We find security, community, in Jesus Christ. In him we find that life has a deeper meaning than the turmoil around us.

This is what the writer of Hebrews is trying to say: "Jesus Christ the same yesterday, and to day, and for ever."

There is something about following Jesus that gives us both a sense of security and a sense of being unified. The disciples were at sea with Jesus one day. A storm arose. Jesus was sleeping in the end of the little boat. Storms on the Sea of Galilee can be ferocious as the winds whistle down the valley between the mountains. So the disciples felt threatened by the storm. They woke Jesus with the question, "Master, carest thou not that we perish?" (Mark 4:38). Jesus arose, rebuked the wind, said to the sea, "Be still." The wind stopped. There was a great calm. Then he said to them, "Why are ye so fearful? how is it that ye have no faith?" "And they feared exceedingly," wanting to know what kind of man this was, that even the sea obeyed him. Here is the source of our calm in the storm of change: Jesus Christ.

When John Wesley was on his way to America, where he failed miserably as a missionary, a storm came up, and it threatened the ship. Passengers and crew were scared and huddled together for a measure of comfort and security. But a little group of people went on with their singing and praying, seemingly oblivious of the storm. John Wesley was intrigued by this demonstration of peace and calm. He discovered that these people were Moravians, who had trusted Christ and committed their lives wholly to him, and so were unafraid in the midst of changing fortunes of a trip.

Cyril Harris wrote a biography of Aaron Burr called *Street of Knives.* A friend of Burr is standing near the front of a boat going down the Mississippi River. Things look dark. The days are tragic. Hugh, the illegitimate son of Burr, strolls toward Blennerhassett and asks if he has lost something. Pointing to the handrail on which they are leaning, Blennerhassett replies that that is what he has lost—something to restrain him when he "goes too near the edge. It has to be strong. Men call it God."

Here is our source of security in change. Arthur Hugh Clough put it in a poem:

> It fortifies my soul to know
> That, though I perish, truth is so:
> That, howsoe'er I stray and range,
> Whate'er I do, Thou dost not change.
> I steadier step when I recall
> That if I slip, Thou dost not fall.

So in the world of whirling change, a world in which we are not sure of anything anymore, where fortunes come and go and men change and friends desert us, there is one thing that does not change: God. "Jesus Christ, the same yesterday, and to day, and for ever."

This makes church membership important. Many people today knock the church and decry its importance. But when the church is what it ought to be, a redemptive fellowship, there is no substitute for it. The community of believers gives support to its members, at the same time inviting others to become a part of this community. Here is a tie that binds. Two men were riding a train. One was an American, the other a foreigner on a visit. They could not converse because they did not understand each other's language. Several attempts at conversation failed. Finally, the American took a New Testament from his pocket. Instantly there was a smile of recognition; a rapport was established. These men had found common ground. This is precisely what the church is supposed to do. It puts solid ground under men's feet when the world is whirling through terrifying changes. Man needs a sense of belonging. Someone has said, "It is lack of unity, of faith, of sense of purpose—this lack of we-ness—which lies at the root of our whole problem." Who said that? It was printed in a report from the United States Department of Health, Education, and Welfare in a discussion of juvenile delinquency. If it is true of youth, it is true of us all. We need to belong to something greater than we are, that will support us and give us a feeling of belonging. The man who tried to assassinate Franklin D. Roosevelt was asked about membership in the church. He replied, "No! No! I belong to nothing, and I suffer!"

Why is membership in the community of believers so important? Rachael Grace Richardson, in "Why I Go to Church," a winning essay in a national contest, wrote: "I go to church because I am human. Being human, I am weak. I am weak in will, weak in purpose, weak in faith. The only sure antidote for my weakness is the Original Source of strength—God. To find him I go to church. Being human, I am lonely. I am lonely for human comradeship; I am lonely for spiritual companionship; I am lonely for Divine Company on my road through life. To find them, I go to church." In any big city, where there are so many people living at loose ends, feeling that none cares or knows, to belong to a church makes good sense. In the church are people who do care, who are interested, people like you, wanting to find the deeper meaning of life. Ralph Sockman tells of receiving a letter from an instructor at the University of Wisconsin. He wrote of Christ Church Methodist, New York: "The courtesy of your congregation is something I shall never forget and I assure you it was no mean factor in helping me keep an anchor in the finer ideals of life. . . . Coming into contact with many people who openly scoffed at things I was fighting to retain as precious, I found your services powerful antidotes to injections of toxins." Jesus put it this way: "Where two or three are gathered together in my name, there am I in the midst of them." This was his way of saying that several Christians together find strength and support and help.

Rolland W. Schloerb points to the church as the source of our strength and peace:

O Church of God, our solitude forsaking,
  We now unite with all who seek thy way—
With those who sing, with those whose hearts are
    breaking,
  We lift our spirits as to God we pray;
O Church of God, our love for thee is waking,
  We bring our alleluias to-day.

O Church of God, like bells at noon-day pealing,
   Thy call has come to us that we may bring
Our strength to serve to all the Christ revealing
   In deeds of love and when our hopes take wing;
O Church of God, where sin and pain find healing,
   To thee our alleluias we sing.

Our Spirit's Home, with joy to thee returning
   Our voices join to sing our highest praise,
For hours of cheer where friendship's fires are burning,
   For strength and peace which gladden all our days;
O Church of God, for thee our hearts are yearning,
   To thee our alleluias we raise.

Finally, the commitment of self to causes that are larger than ourselves, and that make for a sane and decent world, gives us a sense of security and stability. To keep from going crazy, we have to be crazy about something that is worthy of all we are and have. In this way we get our attention from ourselves and onto something bigger than ourselves, and so remove a cause of anxiety and worry and fear. I like to go down near Five Points in Atlanta to look at the statue of Henry W. Grady. Our nation was divided following the Civil War. There was deep depression in the South, and animosity all over the land. Henry W. Grady gave himself to the task of bringing reconciliation. On the monument to him are these words: "He never held or sought public office. When he died he was literally loving the nation into peace."

On an old church in England there is this inscription:

91

"In the year 1653, when all things sacred were throughout the nation either demolished or profaned, Sir Robert Shirley founded this church; whose singular praise it is to have done the best things in the worst times and to have hoped them in the most calamitous."

This is what our Lord meant when he said, "He that is greatest among you shall be your servant." Or, "If any man will come after me, let him deny himself, and take up his cross, and follow me." There are causes bigger than we are that need our help—the causes of brotherhood, of world peace, of declining morality, of the breakdown of the family, of good government locally and nationally, of homeless, hungry, needy boys and girls. A thousand causes beckon to us and ask our help. And many a man has found fulfillment for his Christian life through extending himself to one of these. And somehow our insecurity and our anxiety leave us when we are giving ourselves for something that will outlast us. I listened with awe as six young men and a lovely young lady spoke in our church recently about their love for Christ and told what he has meant to them. They emphasized the fact that in their high school days their one concern had been to be "Mr. It." They wanted to be popular, to have money and cars, play football, and be big shots in the sports field. But once they became Christian, something else dominated their horizon. They wanted only to serve Christ and witness in every possible way to his love. And now their insecurity has disappeared, and they face the future, whether it holds military service, hardship, death even, with one concern: how best to serve Christ and his church. What a testimony! And here is part of the secret of maintaining sanity in a changing world: Get your mind off self, and fix it on Christ, and then give yourself to some service that is greater than you are and that demands all you have.

Three simple things in a recipe for handling the crisis of change: a vital faith in Jesus Christ, vital membership in his church, and vital service to his needy children.

"Remember now thy Creator in the days of thy youth."
—ECCLES. 12:1

~~~~~~~~~~~~~~~~Twelve, Going on Twenty

"I'm No. 77277." "I'm bored." "Getting drafted." "Communicating with people." "Lack of clearly defined moral standards." "The pressure to succeed." "Interpersonal relationships." "I get no satisfaction out of what I'm doing." "What to do with my life." "Want to marry now, and can't." "Don't have any."

The place: Wesley Foundation on a large state university campus. Time: Sunday evening in an informal discussion. The question: What is the major crisis confronting you right now? The question was intended to be personal. There are many social, economic, and political crises confronting all people, but the orientation of these chapters has been very personal, so this question was intended to probe the situation of the individual person. These young people were representative of several areas of the nation, three nationalities, varied walks of life and backgrounds. Their response seems to be about what one would get on any college campus, or from any group of young people anywhere.

As never before, our focus is on youth. This of itself has a bad effect on them. More young people own cars than ever before. They are richer. In fact, young people spend more than ten billion dollars annually on a wide variety of things. There are greater educational opportunities than ever before, and there are more vocational opportunities also. The more than sixty-five million young people under eighteen are in the spotlight. Advertising is beamed to them. Churches and schools talk of doing more for young people. More is planned for them, and more attention given them, than ever before.

By the same token, young people have never felt as insecure as now. Someone has estimated that ten percent of the young of the day have emotional problems. Someone else put the figure at fifty percent. But with all the advances that we have made, there are insecurities and problems.

At no age does an individual feel so insecure as during the years from twelve to twenty. All of us suffer from a sense of insecurity, but youth even more so. The early years have been marked by a feeling of security. They have been comfortable ones in the average home. But the teen-ager is being pushed out gradually, urged to play an increasingly large part in life. He is frightened by what he sees and feels. This accounts for much mutiny and rebellion, loud talk, louder music, and erratic actions. It accounts for much of the fantasy that characterizes youth. Joshua Liebman, in *Peace of Mind,* reminds us: "The adolescent at moments wants to return to that well-loved country of his childhood where there was less competition, where everything was given to him. Every new stage of life is a shattering one emotionally and forces us to build some new adjustment out of broken fragments of our past, out of the precious shards of earlier molds." Bishop Hazen G. Werner, in *Christian Family Living,* writes: "The teen-ager is inarticulate, self-conscious, uneasy with adults, explosive, and inwardly unsure of himself."

It is a strange age. A twelve-year-old went shopping. Her shopping list illustrates some of the drastic changes taking place and some of the confusion. It read: "Water pistol, brassiere, and permanent." Some of the temper of the age is summed up in the ditty "Transfusion" by Nervous Norvus:

> Toolin' down the highway doin' 79
> I'm a twin-pipe poppa,
> And I'm feelin' fine.
> Hey, man, dig that!
> Was that a red stop sign?
> [Sound of crash]
> Transfusion! Transfusion!

One writer in *Daedalus* said, "In many ways, modern American young people seem to walk on eggs more than any generation in the twentieth century." We may not like the music of young people like Bob Dylan, but we'd better listen to what they are saying. I asked a friend recently, "How old is your daughter?" He replied, "Twelve, going on twenty!" We talk a lot about the badness of youth. It is not so much downright badness as it is confusion. Most young people want to know what's right, and will do it. This generation is no worse than any other. We hear more about what they do, and the small minority that goes wrong is louder with it, perhaps. But on college and high school campuses, I get the feeling that most of the students are serious-minded, and have serious intentions about life. We ought to stop trying to prescribe cures for the problems of the young person and set out to understand and accept him. Richard McCann, in *Delinquency: Sickness or Sin?* writes: "It is not sufficient to know the delinquent's deed; we must know the delinquent." A lot is being written of a superficial nature about the problems of youth. Many of us know all too little about the youth himself. But here goes again! What are the crises that confront the modern young person? Let's briefly examine five of them.

First, the pressure to conform. Of course, there are rules that have to be followed. But one temptation that confronts young people is, "Find out what they are thinking, and think it. Find out what they are drinking, and drink it. Find out what they are doing, and do it." Many, if not most, of life's decisions have to be made here. A thousand times the crowd will say, "Aw, come on. Just this once. No one will ever know. It can't hurt

97

you! Don't be a square [or whatever it is you call a square these days]." Several years ago a magazine carried a prayer written to God by a student.

Dear Lord, if we dare to be colorful, if we dare to have character, if we dare to question, if we dare to dissent, or be different, punish us with fire from the pits of hell. Give us a slot in which to conform. We would ask for a place in the shade of the crowd. Keep us passive, hiding our originality and self-expression under mediocrity and nothingness.

Rudyard Kipling summed up the problem of conformity in an interview with Arthur Gordon: "The individual has always had to struggle to keep from being overwhelmed by the tribe. To be your own man is a hard business. If you try it, you'll be lonely often, and sometimes frightened. But no price is too high to pay for the privilege of owning yourself." We are being called a "faceless generation," a generation of "middlebrows." The pressure is on to conform to the crowd.

Second, lack of clearly defined moral standards. This is not peculiar to youth. We all suffer from it. One difficulty for our youth is that adults are preaching nineteenth-century individualism and practicing twentieth-century subsidies; preaching nineteenth-century morality and practicing twentieth-century "new morality." Haskell M. Miller said: "The problem is, in a large measure, one of juveniles in a juvenile society. We talk of mixed-up children. Perhaps we ought also to speak of mixed-up parents." Many of the problems youth face would never occur if children came into the world sincerely wanted. When they know themselves loved, accepted, approved as persons, approved in good things, disciplined fairly when necessary, then youth can face life creatively and honestly. The very society in which we live is not sure of moral standards. Young people are born into a world where morals are neither white nor black, but gray. They need and want guides. A senior in high school said to me recently about her parents: "If only once they would tell me what they think I should do!"

Our present inclination is to do away with standards, rules, and commandments. We are talking about a new morality, and basically the new morality is right. All actions ought to be motivated by love, but which of us is mature enough, even at forty-six, to so decide. We need rules and guidelines as schoolmasters to bring us to the place where our actions can be dictated by love for God and for man, and by a proper respect for ourselves. *Time* has described ours as an era "in which morals are widely held to be both private and relative, in which pleasure is increasingly considered an almost constitutional right rather than a privilege, in which self-denial is increasingly seen as foolishness rather than virtue." This sums up the temper of our age. No wonder youth are confused! Some guides are essential, and there aren't any.

Third, depersonalization. Everybody wants to feel that he is somebody. One boy told me that the only way he could be an individual on the college campus was to bend his ID card. Otherwise, he was No. 77277. Science with its discoveries has taken away much of the feeling of being a person. We are numbers in the Social Security file, "cases" in the doctor's office, "hands" in the factory, "members" of the church.

George A. Buttrick tells a story about Rupert Brooke. The poet was about to sail from Liverpool to New York, and he suddenly felt lonely. It seemed that he was the only passenger without friends at the dock to wave good-bye. Brooke ran down the gangplank, picked out an urchin, and asked, "What's your name?" "Bill," said the boy. "Well, Bill, you are my friend, and here is six-pence. Wave to me when the ship goes." The boy waved a handkerchief in a very grubby hand. We all want to feel that someone cares, that we matter.

Life is lonely at best, but it is made even more so by the depersonalization process of our generation. We are appalled by the bigness of things from factory to college to church. We become ciphers. Every man wents to feel that he is more than a number, somebody, a unique being, a person. A little boy went into a restaurant with his mother and father. When the waitress came, she looked at the little fellow and asked, "What will you have?" He replied, "I'll have a hot dog." Quickly the mother intervened, "Bring him mashed potatoes and roast beef." The waitress paid no attention to the mother, turned back to the boy, and said, "And what do you want on it?" The boy said, "I'll have mustard and catsup." When the waitress was gone, the little fellow pointed to the kitchen and said, "She thinks I'm real!"

And this is the craving of every man—to feel that he is a real person, somebody. To be robbed of that feeling is to experience crisis.

Fourth, the pressure to succeed. A father said to me recently, "No child of mine must fail!" In an atmosphere like that, failure brings inferiority. A student, nervous and upset, came to talk with me. She had failed in school and didn't dare tell her family. "Sue, my older sister, has always made good grades, and I am always compared with her. 'Why can't you be smart like Sue?' they always ask." No wonder she was nervous! Our whole society is guilty of insisting on success. Preachers are always saying, "What a man dreams of doing he can do." But you can't always do that. We must keep up with the Joneses, outdistance the Smiths. There is no place for failure. Psychiatrists know the sad results of insistence on success.

Fifth, how to get along with people. How do you communicate with people—I mean really communicate with them? How do you get along with people happily in a world like ours? The young man, only four years out of college, had already had five jobs. He came to see if he could find out the reason he had been fired so often. I called his former employers, and without exception they said: "He can't get along with people— his secretary, the men at the water cooler, the people in the cafeteria, or anywhere else." Couples come for counseling and say, "We can't communicate." How many people go into life adequately prepared from the standpoint of education, with enough facts and know-how, only to fail miserably because they haven't learned how to get along with people. Individualism is a great thing, but interaction between persons on a satisfying basis is essential to emotional health and success in living. We have learned to fly in the air like birds, to burrow into the ground like moles, to swim in the sea like fish; but, sadly, we haven't learned to walk the earth like men. We live so close together, we live so fast, and there are so many of us, that we have difficulty getting along. Our tempers are short, our patience shorter, the demands upon us greater than ever before. Here in the United States in the old days, if you wanted to travel, you took a stagecoach. If you missed one, there'd be another along in three weeks. But I actually saw a man get angry the other day because he missed a section of a revolving door.

One of the marks of maturity is: Do you have the kind of self-discipline that enables you to work under authority and to work cooperatively with others? The young person is uneasy with adults, and often with other young people, self-conscious, inarticulate, unsure of himself, unsure of others. He wants to be liked, to be approved, to be important to others. Without such approval from others there is crisis. What an opportunity the home and the church have here! In the atmosphere of a right home and a right church, young people learn to respect themselves and to love other people.

There are other crises. What about war? What of the question of race? And what about vocation? Space does

102

not permit a discussion of more of these. What is the answer to crisis in the life of a young person? What help is there?

At least a part of the answer lies in a religious orientation. Many of us have seen reality in the face of Jesus Christ, and are convinced that whoever accepts Christ as his Lord is motivated toward maturity and is helped to meet the crises of life as they come. A young college student told me recently, "Nothing can pressure me to violate what I have been taught all my life." I happen to know some of the things he has been taught: that Jesus Christ is Lord, that God is his father, that men are his brothers, regardless of their color, that the human body is God's temple. The church has meant everything to him, and his parents have given him sensible religious instruction. The crises of campus life come, the major decisions of life confront him, but he has a foundation on which to stand.

Wallace E. Fisher says: "Any person who gives himself to the truth—not in philosophical abstraction or in organizational part, but as it is revealed in the person of Christ—is empowered to live creatively in *any* society." Jesus said, "Ye shall know the truth, and the truth shall make you free." He also said, "I am . . . the truth." Once when Rudyard Kipling was seriously ill, he mumbled a lot in his fever. No one could understand him. But one day his nurse bent over him and asked what he wanted. Kipling replied, "I want God!" That is every man's desire, though not always worded that way. We are created with a desire to worship, to love

103

something greater than ourselves. We never find ourselves until we discover that Someone.

When we have accepted the love of God for ourselves, we can in turn love other people. On the basis of love, insecurity, fear, jealousy, and all else that threatens our very existence can be handled creatively. The desire to be somebody is satisfied through a personal relationship with God. God is personal, alive, and he imparts to us that aliveness that has no other source. Success is measured not in terms of money, or things, or fame, but in terms of doing the will of God, when we are surrendered to him. Inner braces are stronger than outer pressures, and we can withstand the crowd when our relationship with God has become personal. Decisions about life's work, life's mate, and a thousand and one other decisions, large and small, can be made more readily and sensibly when we are in tune with the Creator. A firm faith in God as our friend is a necessary ingredient in handling life's crises. He knows, and he cares.

A second help in handling life's crises is a clearly defined goal in life. Where do you want to go? What do you want to do with the powers God has given you? Real life comes from the conviction that life has significance and is somehow linked to the creative purposes of God. Decide what is important in life for you, regardless of the pressures to conform, and follow after that goal. Dean Alfange said: "I seek opportunity, not security. I do not wish to be a kept citizen, humbled and dulled by having the state look after me. I want to

104

take the calculated risk; to dream and to build, to fail, and to succeed." Viktor Frankl, the Austrian Jewish psychiatrist, describes his experiences in a Nazi death camp in *Man's Search for Meaning*. He wrote that those who gave up were the ones who could see no ultimate meaning to life. They could not see beyond their situation in the camp. And so they died. "The question which beset me was, 'Has all this suffering, this dying around us, a meaning?' For, if not, then ultimately there is no meaning to survival; for a life whose meaning depends upon such a happenstance—whether one escapes or not—ultimately would not be worth living at all." And so every life must have a goal, something worthy of the very best effort and time and ability. To know where you are going, what you want, where you want to come out, makes it easier to meet the crises of life as they come. To have no well-defined purpose creates more crises.

A third thing is involvement—involvement with people. To feel oneself a part of the human race, somehow responsible for others of the race, gives life meaning and direction. Often such a conviction takes strange turns. It may mean taking part in demonstrations, carrying picket signs, protesting. Wherever rights are denied, human personality is fettered, and need exists, there is a place for involvement. A sense of responsibility for working with God and other people to make this world a better place helps make it possible to meet life's crises.

Dietrich Bonhoeffer wrote in one of his letters from prison:

Man is challenged to participate in the sufferings of God at the hands of a godless world. He must, therefore, plunge himself into the life of a godless world, without attempting to gloss over its ungodliness with a veneer of religion or trying to transfigure it. . . . To be a Christian does not mean to be religious in a particular way, to cultivate some particular form of asceticism . . . but to be a man. It is not some religious act which makes a Christian what he is, but participation in the suffering of God in the life of the world. . . . Jesus does not call men to a new religion, but to life.

It is essential that we get involved in the crises of life for the sake of God and other people. One producer of crisis is that we have taken the risks out of life. Someone has defined roughing it as turning down the dial on the electric blanket too low. There are risks to be taken in the world. Jesus was a wise man when he said, "If any man will come after me, let him deny himself, and take up his cross, and follow me" (Matt. 16:24). People in an apartment house can listen to the screams of a dying woman and not help for fear of getting involved, but they will never know the deeper meaning of life. You can insulate self from the crises and hurts and needs of the human race, but those who do so never live. They exist. To lose oneself in the tragedies and the failures and the longings of other people is to find rich meaning, and when one's own crises come along, they are easier to handle.

We have talked about crises in the lives of young people. They come sooner or later to all alike, young and old. But when we are committed to God, when we have a clear-cut goal in life, and when we are involved in the hurts and needs of other people, somehow we are equipped to handle our own crises when they do come. "Remember now thy Creator in the days of thy youth."

"Nay, in all these things we are more than conquerors through him that loved us." —Rom. 8:37

What on Earth Is God Doing in the World?

A question on the lips of people who suffer pain, or loss, or anguish in another form, is Why? Why were 130 lives snuffed out suddenly, with no warning, in an airplane crash? Why must families and friends be subjected to such torment and anxiety and sorrow? Why can't we have a world without tragedy? Why does God allow war, disease, death, pain? What on earth is God doing in the world? These are a few of the thousands of questions asked beginning, Why? We ought to think deeply about the matter and arrive at some conclusions that will help us when our own sorrow comes.

Our concern is not just for our own suffering. G. A.

Studdert-Kennedy, a British chaplain in World War I, said that any person who was undisturbed by the pain and suffering of others was himself suffering from "hardening of the heart or softening of the brain." Suffering is a universal problem. It confronts us daily, brought sharply into focus by one tragedy after another. It is a part of life. Job reminds us that "man is born unto trouble, as the sparks fly upward" (Job 5:7).

"God doesn't care! My husband has been a good man all his life. He has worked hard, been a good churchman, taught a Sunday school class, has been honest and kind. He never knowingly turned away a person in need. Now he has to die young, while people who have never done anything for anybody, have never been to church, have cheated and lied, live on. Why? It just is not fair!" she cried as she buried her face in her hands.

Therein lies a problem that has confronted men since first they began to think. Why does a good man suffer? We seem to have the answer to the question, Why does a bad man suffer? He deserves it, we say. He has brought it upon himself. But what of this good man? The Old Testament is very definite in its ideas that goodness and righteousness are rewarded by prosperity and good health and long life, while sinfulness causes a man affliction and hardship. This is the reasoning behind the book of Job, and a theory which Job exploded because he was a righteous man and yet suffered. Why does any man suffer?

No more wonderful person ever lived than Catherine Booth. She was devoted to her husband, her children. Yet she found time to go into the slums of the city of London and help the unfortunate, save the sick, the lost. She encouraged her husband to leave the Methodist Church rather than have his call to serve circumscribed by regulations. She was one of the front-runners in the organization of the Salvation Army. No one can estimate the good she has done. And yet when she came to the day of her death, she said that she could not recall one day when she had been free from pain! Why?

Fanny Crosby had done nothing wrong. In fact, she was a mere child of six when she lost her sight through an accident. Why?

"He has cancer! If God cared, he could stop cancer!"

During the last war, I got a letter from a mother whose son had been killed in service. "I never intend to step into another church. The church lied to me. It has fooled me into believing what isn't so. I have been taught that if you prayed, you'd get an answer. I prayed that my boy would come home safely. Now he is dead. I hate God! You just can't trust him!"

On June 3, 1963, a jet rolled down the runway at Orly Field in Paris. On board were 132 people. Some of them were known to me as committed Christians. Most, perhaps all, of them were religious people. In the twinkling of an eye, there was a sickening crash, a fire, and 130 people were dead. Why?

There are three basic causes for suffering in our world.

The impartial operation of the laws of God makes a cosmos out of what would otherwise be chaos. The laws of God operate for the good and the bad alike. If God should suspend the natural laws that operate for one man for one minute, every other living creature in the world would be killed instantly. Here is the law of gravity. It is no respecter of persons. A good man climbs a mountain. He has been a Christian all his life. He is active in the church. He loses his footing. He falls a thousand feet to his death. The fact that he had an outstanding record in living made no difference at all to the law of gravity. It works for good and bad alike. There is no distinction. In this case, its working caused a tragedy.

On February 26, 1844, one of the great disasters of naval history took place on the Potomac River. The "Princeton," a powerful warship, was taking some members of Congress for a trip. On board also were the President of the United States, the Secretary of the Navy, the Secretary of State, and others. To show the power of the new boat and her guns, one of the largest guns was fired. The second time the gun burst, killing both the secretaries of Navy and State and several other men of distinction. Here is a strange thing. Just before the fatal shot, Senator Thomas Benton of Missouri felt a hand on his shoulder, and as he stepped back to speak to the man, Secretary of the Navy Gilmore slipped into the place he had vacated. At that instant the gun went off, and the Secretary was killed. Soon afterward, Senator Benton, who had quarreled with Daniel Webster, sought out the man and wanted a reconciliation: "It seemed to me, Mr. Webster," said Benton, "as if that touch on my shoulder was the hand of the Almighty stretched down there, drawing me away from what otherwise would have been instantaneous death. That one circumstance has changed the whole current of my thought and life. I feel that I am a different man; and I want, in the first place, to be at peace with all those with whom I have been so sharply at variance."

What kind of crazy thinking is that? We wonder that a man with enough brains to be elected to the United States Senate could be so shallow in his thinking. What kind of God would slip Benton out of place to save him, and slip Gilmore into his place to kill him? What kind of weak God is ours if he saved Benton and could not have saved Gilmore too—or, for that matter, the whole crowd? The truth is, there was a mechanical defect in the gun, and the physical laws of the universe, operating for all alike, caused it to blow up.

Take the matter of cancer, so much in our thinking these days. Cancer comes not as punishment of God for wrong. It comes because something in the natural laws of God has gone wrong with the human body. I must turn aside here a moment to defend the character of God. Not that he needs any defense, but I can't keep still any longer. People are always saying to me, "I must bear up under this, for I know it is God's will." Or, "God took my son, and I must accept it as his will for me." I was in a room not long ago when a man died. His family, members of a church, bore up bravely under the loss, but said something that I can never accept. They said, "It is God's will that he go like this. We will accept his will." What kind of God is that? We talk about God as our Father, and we give him all the attributes of a good earthly father. Which earthly father, to punish his child, would send an incurable disease upon that child? Or which earthly father, to punish a wife with whom he was at odds, would kill one of their children? Even Job's suffering was brought on by the devil. The devil carried out the provisions of the contract. Paul's thorn was a "messenger of Satan to buffet me" (II Cor. 12:7). You see, we accuse God of things that the lowest human being would not do. He does not deliberately send into our lives any tragedy that would bring us suffering or pain.

It is the will of God that we be healthy, happy, and that this world of ours be a paradise. In that sense, he has exactly the same will for each of us. The impartial operation of God's laws brings suffering. Only in this sense can you say suffering is the will of God.

The interdependence of people brings suffering also. There are nearly two hundred million of us in the United States. We live together more closely than men have ever lived before. None of us would want to live like Robinson Crusoe on a lonely island, though many mornings when I get up, I have the urge to hie me away to some island paradise and be alone for awhile.

Because we live together and are so interdependent, we suffer.

Here is a couple driving down the highway, obeying the traffic laws, enjoying the beauty of the countryside. Suddenly, from out of nowhere, there comes a car, driven at dizzying speed by a man under the influence of alcohol. He hits their car; one of them is killed, and the other spends painful months in the hospital. Why did two innocent people suffer? Because this is an interdependent world. When the man got drunk and then got over on the wrong side of the road, he was breaking rules that were made so that people might live happily together in this world. People tell me every day that it is all right to drink, that it is a personal matter. And yet the records reveal that in a large majority of the wrecks last year, whiskey was involved. According to the FBI, more than half the arrests in any year are caused by alcohol, or crime directly involving liquor law violations. We are living in a land where the alcohol ritual is more important than the church ritual. And we pay for it, very often the innocent paying a higher price than the guilty.

Take the matter of war. Your son may have been called upon to sacrifice his life because there are tyrants in the world who threaten the well-being of all mankind. It is not God's will that our world be drenched in blood every twenty-five years. Wars come because men are at odds with God, with themselves; because of evil, tangled motives, selfish desires, an overemphasis on nationalism. It is not God's will that

114

the horsemen of the apocalypse ride roughshod over the earth bringing in their wake hunger, disease, ignorance, hate. We live as interdependent people, and what we do as individuals and as nations affects all other people everywhere. If we only lived in isolation— but we don't. Much of our suffering comes because of our interdependence.

Our freedom of choice causes suffering also. God made us free to choose our own way. A man decides that he can beat an express train to a crossing, and misses by only one second. A man decides that he can take a drink and stop, forgetting that the first calls for a second, then a third. He winds up in jail with a murder rap, and he never knew when he committed the murder! The Japanese decide to attack Pearl Harbor, and two nations that have been friends for years are at war. Evil men decide that Jesus Christ is a threat to their way of life, so he must go. The cross follows. A boy decides to go into a far country; a father's heart breaks. A girl with every opportunity in the world to make good, a leader in high school with a chance to go to college, has to get married instead; the hearts of a father and mother break as they see their dreams disappear. A man decides that he can live a sinful life and get by. You see, God has made us free. We can choose, and we have the same privilege of making a wrong choice as of making a right one.

God does not—yes, cannot—intervene in these things for one against another. He is no respecter of persons. If in the body of a good man something gets crossways and does not act as God intended from creation that it should act, cancer, tuberculosis, or some other disease sets in. A man in ignorance makes a wrong decision. God does not step in to take away the consequences. A man sins, and moral laws operate impartially. "Whatsoever a man soweth, that shall he also reap." The natural laws of the world, the law of interdependence, the law of free choice—all operate for good and bad, rich and poor, black and white alike.

But I must emphasize over and over that the intentional will of God for his creation is that every person be happy, healthy, and successful in his own way and to the limit of his ability. God planned a great world. He intended that it be a paradise. But because of man's willful sin, his ignorance, his interdependence, and because of the impartial operation of natural laws, man finds himself in a world that is far from a paradise. It is not God's will for man that he suffer, live in degrading circumstances, fight like a beast, drink like a madman, distort values, and inflict suffering on others. This is man's doing and not God's.

God paid man a compliment in two ways: He gave him freedom of choice, and he made man the only one of his creatures that can ask about life's ultimate meaning. Animals feel pain, but they do not raise questions about it. Man asks, "Why did this happen to me?" Both these facts serve to deepen man's sense of suffering.

What God does not will, he can use. It is not so much why we suffer as how we suffer. Good and bad suffer.

The laws of nature, of interdependence, of free choice being what they are, all men suffer. A good God cannot show partiality between men, even between saint and sinner. How we suffer is the important thing. We can use the experience to become embittered toward life, or we can use it to build strong, great character. Job came through suffering, which his so-called friends thought was brought on by sin, saying, "Though he slay me, yet will I trust in him." Take the case of Fanny Crosby again. God did not will her blindness. It was an accident. It happened because certain natural laws were broken. But the accident having occurred, God could use Fanny Crosby to write,

> Jesus, keep me near the cross;
> There a precious fountain,
> Free to all, a healing stream,
> Flows from Calvary's mountain.

Dozens of other hymns by that same Christian woman have literally lifted men's souls up to heaven. When we suffer, no matter what the cause, and can have such a faith, we are on the road to rugged good character and everlasting life.

A woman, returning from the doctor, where she had learned that she had cancer and would not live many months, said to her friend, "Oh, I wish I had never been made!" The friend, being of deeper understanding, replied, "You have not been made. You are being made now." The sandalwood tree scents the axe that cuts it down. In Revelation are the words, "What are these

117

which are arrayed in white robes? And whence came they? . . . These are they which came out of great tribulation, and have washed their robes . . . in the blood of the Lamb" (Rev. 7:13-14.) This is a letter written by John to people living under great stress and suffering. He is saying to them that if they are faithful, if they are true to God, *in spite of their sufferings,* they shall at the last inherit a crown of life. Their names are written in the Lamb's Book of Life! Nothing is said in this great book about why men suffer, but it is filled with messages about how men suffer. Someone said recently, "I'm proud to be trusted with cancer." Nietzsche said, "Whoever has a reason for living endures almost any mode of life." Suffering can be used as a part of life's schooling. God does not will evil for any one of us; but things being what they are, he allows it. Parents don't will that a child fall down and bump his head as he learns to walk; but they allow it, else how will he ever learn? So God can use what he does not choose, evil and suffering, to make us stronger and greater characters.

Having seen some of the reasons why men suffer, and having decided that it is not why we suffer but how we suffer, we arrive at this final point: God is good, and God is with us in our suffering, to help us accept it and then use it to build greater character. We do not have to bear any experience in life alone. Our own strength is not sufficient. Jesus demonstrated man's need for God in the dark hours of life; then he went on to demonstrate that man can have God in these hours.

Before his hour of greatest suffering he went alone into the garden of Gethsemane to pray. And in the silences of that garden he got strength to say: "Not my will, but thine, be done" (Luke 22:42). And on the cross in his desperate hour of need, he cried out, "Father, into thy hands I commend my spirit" (Luke 23:46). He was able to bear the sorrows of rejection, his physical pain, death itself, because he lived close to God and availed himself of the power of God. Every man can do likewise. It is not enough to wait until suffering comes, or sorrow reaches its hands into our homes, to begin building strength and preparing against the day. Every day must be a day of preparation, so that when these things come, we can know the truth in God's word to Paul: "My grace is sufficient for thee" (II Cor. 12:9).

Bishop James Pike reminds us forcefully that many people wrestle with their problems alone and never take God into account. He says that people like this are trying to put a jigsaw puzzle together with some mighty important pieces missing. When we try to explain suffering or bear it without God, there is a great void, a blank place at the center of life. It is faith in God that makes it possible for us to bear up under suffering and use our suffering to build character. It is not enough to say, "Buck up, old boy; keep a stiff upper lip!" A stiff upper lip can become mighty limp. We need to lay hold again on the great affirmations of our faith, chief of which is "I believe in God," for such faith transforms us. Listen to some words from the Word:

119

Who shall separate us from the love of Christ? shall tribulation, or distress, or persecution, or famine, or nakedness, or peril, or sword? . . . Nay, in all these things we are more than conquerors through him that loved us. For I am persuaded, that neither death, nor life, nor angels, nor principalities, nor powers, nor things present, nor things to come, nor height, nor depth, nor any other creature, shall be able to separate us from the love of God, which is in Christ Jesus our Lord. (Rom. 8:35, 37-39.)

John Greenleaf Whittier sums up the faith of the Christian in "The Eternal Goodness" when he says:

> O Friends! with whom my feet have trod
>   The quiet aisles of prayer,
> Glad witness to your zeal for God
>   And love of man I bear. . . .
>
> Yet, in the maddening maze of things,
>   And tossed by storm and flood,
> To one fixed trust my spirit clings;
>   I know that God is good! . . .
>
> I know not what the future hath
>   Of marvel or surprise,
> Assured alone that life and death
>   His mercy underlies.
>
> And if my heart and flesh are weak
>   To bear an untried pain,
> The bruisèd reed He will not break,
>   But strengthen and sustain. . . .

And Thou, O Lord! by whom are seen
    Thy creatures as they be,
Forgive me if too close I lean
    My human heart on Thee!

I read somewhere a fine statement about the great Victorian general, Charles George Gordon. On the Sunday before he left for the Sudan, General Gordon went all around London to a number of churches, taking Communion as many times as he possibly could—in order, he said, to start out "brim full of God." Brim full of God! This is the secret of "bearing" suffering, of accepting it, of understanding it, and of using it. Apart from God, there is no answer to the "why?" of sorrow and pain and suffering.

William Stidger once told a story about how people brim full of God handle suffering.

During World War II, a family received two telegrams in two weeks announcing that their sons had both been killed in action. This family had always been active Christians, involved in church affairs very deeply. It was near Easter, and there was much speculation about what they would do on Easter. The congregation was not surprised. They appeared in their regular places when the worship hour came, faces drawn in grief, but with a look of victory in their eyes. However, it remained for a small boy in that congregation to say the ultimate word which summed up that beautiful and dramatic experience. He was sitting in the pew immediately behind that father and mother.

Naturally, the boy had heard all the town gossip, speculation, and wonder about whether that family would come to church on Easter morning. Therefore he kept his eye on them every minute of that solemn service. He saw them open their hymnbooks, rise, and sing with the rest of the congregation. He saw them bow their heads reverently when the pastor prayed. He saw that they were listening intently and responding fervently to the responsive Bible reading of the morning, which was a triumphant lesson about Christ having risen from the dead and redeemed all human life from death. The boy's small face looked puzzled. Then came the collection, and as it passed those parents, his keen boy eyes saw that the father, whom he knew to be a comparatively poor man, put a crisp new ten-dollar bill on the plate as if he had not already given more than his share, in giving his sons. It was more than this boy's curiosity could stand in one morning, and he pulled his father, who sat beside him, down and whispered with awe and boy reverence into his father's ear: "Dad, they must *believe* it!"

The father, not catching clearly that small boy's whispered word, asked, "What do you mean, son?" "Why, they must actually believe in Easter. They're here: they sang, they read the Bible; and what's more they gave—gosh—ten dollars. Dad, they must believe in Easter!"

The sufferer can do many things that are good: show courage, be cheerful, speak a good word for Jesus Christ, pray. He can, instead of whining, transform life

122

into a veritable garden of beauty and of helpfulness. Kierkegaard insisted that suffering is instrumental to a great life: "The way of purification is in affliction." Many people, because of their glorious reaction to suffering and pain, have hewn out of hard stone grace, beauty, and character.

Take your suffering. Know that God is with you. Trust him completely. Use suffering gloriously. Make it a character builder. Use it for God. God has shown us in Jesus Christ that his purpose for his creation is love. He planned from the start a world that is good. That world will ultimately be. It is not so important why you suffer, as how you suffer. God did not will that any suffer and perish, but that all might come to a knowledge of him and be useful and happy. With his grace and love, we can use even pain and suffering for greatness.

"And even to your old age I am he; and even to hoar hairs will I carry you: I have made, and I will bear." —Isa. 46:4

"Grow Old Along with Me! The Best Is ~~~~~~~~~~~~Yet to Be" — Says Who?

There are now fourteen million people in the United States over sixty-five. And the number is increasing by four hundred thousand every year. The only way to keep from getting old is to die young. If you live, you'll someday be old, at least in years. Many people think old age is a disease, something to be thwarted if possible. But someone has said that if any period is a disease, it is youth. Age is recovering from it. One woman said to her psychiatrist: "The happiest day of my life was the day I stopped trying to look twenty years younger than I am and decided to be myself." John Barrymore was asked once if acting was as much fun at seventy as it was at forty. He replied, "Nothing is as much fun at seventy as it was at forty!"

While the years after sixty-five may not be as glamorous as those before, they can be rewarding, happy, and productive. We ought not just grow old gracefully, but creatively, helpfully, and hopefully.

Of course, there are minus signs with increasing years. Crises come. There is failing health, loss of eyesight and hearing. We lose our own teeth. Our physical strength lessens. A man over sixty-five was talking to a friend about his tennis game. He said, "My brain barks out the commands to my body: Run forward rapidly. Start now. Slam the ball over the net. Run quickly back and get ready to do it again!" "What happens?" the friend asked him. "Then," the older man replied slowly, "my body says, 'Who, me?'" Friends die, and there is an increasing loneliness. A husband or wife dies, and life seems empty. The children grow up, marry, move away, and there is a feeling of purposelessness. Diminished income makes it necessary to cut expenses. Sometimes old age means moving from a loved home. But the greatest crisis in later years is the lack of purpose for living. Many times an older person has plenty to live on, someone to live with, but nothing to live for. William James said that "the deepest drive in human nature is to be appreciated." Often the older person feels neglected, unwanted, and unnecessary. Science is lengthening life expectancy. Unless ways can be found to increase the purpose for living, science is not doing us a favor, but only creating more crises.

Many times when a person reaches the deadline at sixty-five, it is his own fault. Henry David Thoreau

125

said, "The boy gathers material for a temple, and when he is thirty builds a woodshed." Life makes demands of us, and if we meet them, we never get old. Years accumulate, but we never get old. Growing old is a contradiction. Being old is the stage where one stops growing. To equate age and number of years is a mistake. Some people are old at twenty. They have already stopped growing. A man of thirty told me the other day that he hadn't read a book in five years. He is already old.

I came on some interesting figures recently. Someone estimated that 64 percent of the great achievements of the human race were made by people over sixty; 23 percent between the ages of seventy and eighty; and only 13 percent by those under forty. Moses enlisted for his greatest job at eighty. He died at 120, and his biographer said of him, "His eye was not dim, nor his natural force abated" (Deut. 34:7). John Wesley preached right up to the time of his death at ninety. Michelangelo said at seventy, "I am learning." George Meuller volunteered for the mission field at sixty-five and for seventeen years made extensive trips around the world. He traveled more than two hundred thousand miles between his seventieth and eighty-seventh birthdays, and spoke more than five thousand times. Milton wrote *Paradise Lost* when he was in his late fifties. When he was seventy, E. Stanley Jones wrote the mission board: "You, of course, have to retire me according to the rules, at seventy. You may retire me as a missionary of the Board. But you cannot retire me as a missionary and as an evangelist. That goes on. And goes on clear up to the very end." Bishop Arthur J. Moore, resident bishop of the Atlanta Area of The Methodist Church for twenty years, retired at seventy-two according to church law. He is now seventy-eight, and since retirement has preached in 170 or more revivals and preaching missions. He carries a heavier schedule than most of my friends half his age. One of the great men of The Methodist Church that I have known is Dr. Lester Rumble. Before he retired at a recent session of our annual conference, he was serving North Decatur Methodist Church, a vital, growing suburban congregation. He was assigned to this post at seventy. One of the members of his official board said of him, "He is the best thing that ever happened to us!"

What Emerson said in his *Journal* makes good sense for us as we consider the later years in life: "Do not waste yourself in rejection; do not bark against the bad, but chant the beauty of the good." A positive attitude, an attitude of faith, can transform fears about old age into anticipation and expectation. The crises of increasing years can be dissolved. Antique dealers have a slogan: "The older the better." A man in New York owns a cabinet made from the wood of an old sailing vessel. With age—more than one hundred years now—its pores have contracted and its colors deepened until it is a thing of rare beauty. This ought to happen to every living soul. The increasing years ought to increase wisdom, kindness, affection, and faith. "Grow old along with me! The best is yet to be"—this ought to be the

127

affirmation of every person. What a way to live! The man who lives with optimism never reaches the limit.

Some ministers say, "My congregation is predominantly young adults and youths. Why preach to them on old age?" That's simple. People accumulate years, faster than they realize. You don't wait until you get there to begin getting ready to live. To be a gracious, kindly, helpful, happy, useful person at sixty-five, you have to begin at zero. A woman came to Emerson and asked at what age she ought to start teaching her child manners and morals and truth. Emerson asked how old the child was. The mother replied, "Three years." Emerson said, "You are three years late!" The kind of person you will be at sixty-five or seventy-five is being hammered out right now at ten, or fifteen, or twenty. So let me suggest some things that will help us use the later years in life, things that we can begin to do, whether we are young or have many years already.

Don't ever close your mind. Never stop learning. John Locke said, "It is a duty we owe to God to have our minds constantly open to receive and entertain new truth when we meet it." The number of years does not confer an honorary degree for wisdom. A man can be as stupid at sixty-five as he was at twenty-five. And he will be if he does not keep his mind open and alert. Old age is a way of life, a question of intensity and not of duration. Other things being equal, those who live the longest are those who think the best thoughts, who keep their minds stimulated with fresh ideas, and who draw from inner resources a sort of vital fire which preserves energies through the years. E. Stanley Jones tells of a woman 104 years old. She had been a missionary in Burma. Every day she read her Bible aloud in Burmese. She said, "I don't want to lose the accent." She wanted to be able to talk with her Burmese friends when she got to heaven. Our bodies sag because our minds are sagging. We take it for granted that as we get older we lose the ability to learn and think. Nothing is further from the truth. Rather, we lose the willingness to make the effort to learn and think. John Wesley wrote in his *Journal* at seventy-one: "I find just the same strength as I did thirty years ago. . . . My sight is considerably better now, and my nerves firmer than they were then. . . . I have none of the infirmities of old age, and have lost several I had in my youth." Don't ever close your mind. Keep learning. Keep growing.

Keep abreast of the times. Don't just live in the past. Memories are wonderful, and we could not live without the experiences of yesterday. You cannot live today, nor can you adequately prepare for tomorrow, without the wisdom of yesterday. But to live in the past and be content with what happened then is fatal. Suppose you are sixty-five, and one evening you are talking with friends. Suddenly you realize that all you are saying is, "My mother used to say. . . ." Or, "Grandpa told us. . . ." Or, "I remember when I was a boy. . . ." Take the heel of your hand, place it gently under your chin, push your mouth shut, and hold it there until you can think of something more up-to-date to say. To be a bore is bad at any age. But to be an old bore is unforgivable. Keep up with what is happening in the world. Kagawa used to pray, 'May I never be guilty of yawning at life." The only difference between a rut and a grave is the depth. Life gets boring for us and we get boring for everybody unless we keep up with what is happening in the world. Be able to talk politics, medicine, space exploits, cars, knitting, painting, latest books, the Book of books. Keep up with the times. A tractor salesman went to see a farmer who still plowed with a mule. He put on his best sales pitch. When he finished, the farmer replied, "I've been studying the likes and dislikes, the tastes, of the mule for forty years, and I don't intend to throw all that knowledge over for any newfangled tractor!" This is the attitude that makes us old. It is a tragedy that you can write the biography of most people for one day, then multiply it by 365 and then by seventy years, and you have it. Keep up with the times. Stay interested in what is happening every day.

Keep busy. Retirement comes early for most people now. Policies requiring retirement at sixty-five are enforced in almost all businesses. It is not enough that we have learned to make a living. Our professional skills may be of little value to us when retirement comes. While we are making a living with our chosen profession, we ought also to be learning other ways to be useful. Many a man dies of boredom after he retires. Many a wife laments at her husband's retirement that she married him for better or worse, but not for lunch every day. We need to feel needed. While getting on toward the time of retirement, begin to think of ways to continue to be useful. It may be that you can use what you have done all your life. I know a carpenter who, when he retired, set up a workshop in his basement; and now he gives lessons every afternoon to the neighborhood kids in cabinetmaking. A minister retired and, instead of quitting, moved with his wife to a little community where they had been preaching only once a month. They bought a house, and he got permission of his district superintendent to begin services in the church every Sunday. He reorganized the Sunday school, and now is a vital, happy part of a community and is living as fully and well as he ever did. Elton Trueblood talks of your "other vocation." How many places of service there are in the church for retired men and women! Rollin Walker said once that age does not destroy the power to pray. Youth needs encouragement from a wiser, older person. And today there are countless opportunities through organizations like the Golden Age clubs for part-time employment, for recreation, for friendships. As the years pile up, learn to do some things you will enjoy doing, and profit from doing them the rest of your life.

Believe in yourself. It is fatal to say, "I'm not worth anything to God or man." Life has a worthwhile goal for every man regardless of the years. We are made in God's image, and he needs us as long as we live. We get rebellious because we can't see or hear or chew as well as we once could. We must adjust to these in-

131

firmities and keep going. Edwin Markham put it beautifully on his eightieth birthday.

> I am done with the years that were: I am quits:
>   I am done with the dead and old.
> They are mines worked out: I delved in their pits.
>   I have saved their grain of gold.
>
> Now I turn to the future for wine and bread:
>   I have bidden the past adieu.
> I laugh and lift hand to the years ahead:
>   "Come on: I am ready for you!"

Some people live and succeed with almost unbelievable handicaps. A newspaper carried the story some time ago about a young man who had been wounded in the war. He had lost one arm above the elbow, and the other just below. Both legs were gone. What chance in this world did he have to do anything? If you had seen him right after he was wounded, you would have said, "He'll be a hopeless invalid the rest of his life." Today he is running a farm, doing some of the work himself. It is an unbelievable achievement, but true. Certainly increasing years bring weakness, failure in many ways, but we are still important to God and man. There's purpose for every life, and God can use us as long as we live for his glory and for the good of mankind. Never forget who you are, or what you cost, or why you are here, or where you are going.

Keep developing friendships. Our old ones leave us. Someone asked an old man if he had any enemies. He replied that he didn't have a one. Asked to explain why, he said simply, "I've outlived them." We outlive friends and enemies. We find ourselves sitting with television and radio, alone day after day, simply because we let our friendships get in poor repair. Charles Lamb used to moan, "I have had playmates, I have had companions, in my days of childhood, in my joyful school days. All, all have gone, the old familiar faces." And that had happened to him because he didn't make any new ones. Samuel Johnson said, "If a man does not make new acquaintances as he advances through life, he will soon find himself alone. A man, sir, must keep his friendships in constant repair." Don't wait for people to come to you. Go where they are. We can never afford to dispense with the little niceties of life. We need tact, pleasantness, interest in other people all our lives. One old woman insisted that she had earned the right to be ugly and disagreeable, and that it was the duty of her children to put up with it because of the love and sacrifice she had showered on them. To have friends, be one. Make them wherever you can—church, Golden Age Club, neighborhood. Friends are all around us for the cultivating.

Be wholly surrendered to God. Tagore has an old man say, "I am getting old now, so I depend more on the wind than the oars—my sails are set." As the years increase, our dependence upon God becomes more and more important. It is a tragedy at any age not to live close to God and draw on his abundant available power. But with increasing age, we need him more than ever.

133

Howard Whitman, in *A Reporter in Search of God,* tells of his travels about the country asking questions of people about their faith. One woman told him that she did not expect to be delivered from troubles because she was a Christian. Whitman asked her what she did expect. She replied that she expected to have power to meet them when they came. We save money for retirement; we find a home and try to have it paid for; we make sure our Social Security papers are in order; we watch our diet and health. How unimportant these are if we neglect the one source of power and hope and usefulness: God. More often than not, the tragedy of old age is emptiness. But when God is our stay, there is no emptiness. Life is full right up to the very end. Roselle Mercier Montgomery's poem, "On the Death of an Aged Friend," has some lines that I frequently use at funerals:

> You took life, tiptoe, to the very last;
> It never lost for you its lovely look;
> You kept your interest in its thrilling book.

That is made possible when we walk with the Lord, in the light of his love. Bishop Edwin Holt Hughes came to retirement after a long and illustrious ministry in the church. In his address at retirement, he said in part:

For my remaining years I seek no vacation. Having cultivated the art of preparation and having been in love with toil, I feel that I must not cease. Perhaps your release of me from one kind of work will permit me to do more of another kind. I have had a happy life, so very, very happy. For thirty years the Shepherd has led me through sunshine with scarcely a cloud. When I did go into the valley of the shadow, he was with me to comfort with his rod and staff. Now he grants me this solemnly joyful hour. I beg you to continue to give me your love. I could not live without it, since you have made me so used to its climate.

How could a man at retirement be so joyful and optimistic? Simple. He had walked with the Savior across the years of his life and had made preparation for the coming of retirement and old age. The writer of Ecclesiastes gives some good advice when he says, "Remember now thy Creator in the days of thy youth, while the evil days come not, nor the years draw nigh, when thou shalt say, I have no pleasure in them" (12:1). Here is where preparation for a happy, useful, cheerful old age begins.

David Livingstone came to the University of Glasgow to receive an honorary degree. Usually the students hissed and booed persons coming for this purpose, but they were silent as this gaunt man took his place on the platform. Livingstone had an arm hanging helplessly by his side, mangled by a lion in Africa. He had had jungle fever dozens of times as he went about his work. His beloved Mary had died in the jungle. He stood and talked about his work. He told how he had opened up new trade for Great Britain, and how he had preached and taught and worked with the natives. He told them he was going back. Then he asked if they

135

knew what had sustained him in the years he had been there, and what would give him strength to go back again. There was silence. Then Livingstone said, "Long ago I heard the whisper in the ear, 'Lo, David, I am with you alway, even unto the end of the age.'" This is the source of our power, our ability, to accept change and disappointment. This power gives us strength to keep right on making a contribution to life as long as we live. This power enables us to be cheerful, get along with family and friends, pray, be pleasant, be good. This power enables us to endure to the end, to fight the good fight of faith, and to obtain the victory. This power enables us to face death with faces alight with anticipation.

A little boy wrote a letter to Walter Russell Bowie. He closed the letter with this line: "I hope you live all your life!"

"He was there alone."   —MATT. 14:23
"I am not alone, because the Father is with me."—JOHN 16:32

I Wish to God I Didn't Feel
~~~~~~~~~~~~~~~~~~~~~~~~~~~~~~~~~~~~~~~So Lonely

The telephone rang. When I said "hello," a male voice said, "I wish to God I didn't feel so lonely! You'd think in a city like Atlanta loneliness would be impossible. Loneliness is worse than sickness!"

One of the frequent chapel speakers in the seminary said in a sermon, "The loneliest place in the world is Five Points at noon." I had recently come to Atlanta, but I had been at Five Points at noon. Thousands of people surged through this confluence of five major traffic arteries in search of a place to eat or park. I thought he was jesting. But now, having been a minister in a big city for more than twenty years, I know he was right. I also know what he meant. Loneliness is an inner state. One may experience loneliness in its worst form in a crowd.

Men have always faced this problem. The psalmist cried:

> Turn thou to me, and be gracious to me;
>   for I am lonely and afflicted. (Ps. 25:16 RSV.)

Odell Shepherd talks of "the dull ache of loneliness," and we understand. In reply to my question, "How are you this morning?" a man said recently, "I feel fine, but I'm lonely." Loneliness lies in wait for every man, and we must find a way to handle this crisis. In reviewing Harry Stack Sullivan's book, *The Interpersonal Theory of Psychiatry,* Rollo May made the observation that "there are many indications that we in the middle decades of the twentieth century are moving into the age of loneliness. The barometer portends that if we survive at all we are likely to live in chilly times, when it will be difficult to feel real warmth and meaning in our relations with our fellow man."

There are many causes of loneliness. Look at some of the major ones.

Paul Tillich says, "Man is alone because he is man." God made us this way, separated from all other bodies. Man is destined to live alone. The Spanish philosopher, Ortega y Gasset, has pictured the solitary nature of man's life: "Each man is an island in that he lives and dies in the solitude of his own consciousness." When the German writer Novalis said, "Every Englishman is an island," he was being critical. But what he said is true of every man. No one can ever fully enter into the life of another. Just having people around may mean only an accumulation of lonely people. To have a date, or drink with buddies, or have lunch with a group is not necessarily a cure for loneliness. Man's loneliness is a mark of his greatness. It places a responsibility upon each man that none other can shoulder for him. He can look at his world in a way that none other can. His loneliness is a mark of freedom. No one can finally violate a man's personality unless that man wills it so. It is tragic when this private world is lost to us by the pressures of people around us. Loneliness is at once a mark of greatness and a matter of grave crisis.

Sin is another cause of loneliness. Rudyard Kipling, in "Tomlinson," wrote: "The sin ye do by two and two ye must pay for one by one." Sin makes a man lonely simply because it separates a man from God, from his best self, and often from his fellow human beings. Adam and Eve disobeyed God and they "hid themselves" (Gen. 3:8). The Bible almost begins with an account of Cain killing Abel. God said to Cain, "A fugitive and a vagabond shalt thou be in the earth" (Gen. 4:12). In the year 1602, a pamphlet appeared at Leiden in Holland, telling of a Jew who had poked fun at Jesus as he walked the Via Dolorosa, carrying the cross. The Jew shouted, "Go quicker!" Jesus stopped to answer him, "I go, but thou shalt wait till I return." This tale of the wandering Jew struck the fancy of men everywhere, and the story has been told in fiction and poetry. It is legend, but it illustrates a great truth. Sin separates and makes lonely.

Loneliness may result from inward emptiness. This is one of the greatest problems confronting us as human beings today. T. S. Eliot knew what he was talking about when he wrote,

> We are the hollow men
> We are the stuffed men
> Leaning together
> Headpiece filled with straw. Alas!

We do not have great convictions, or high standards, or a final authority inside ourselves to which we turn for direction. I asked a young woman about her faith one day, and she said, "I believe everything a little bit." I am sure she meant that she found help in many philosophies and religions, but she was giving voice to a confused emptiness that characterizes the life of far more people than we know. Who among us has a keen sense of the importance and worth of life? Who has a sense of direction, a source of power that is never failing? No wonder our nerves drive us crazy. A patient said to Carl Jung, "If only I knew that my life had some meaning and purpose, then there would be no silly story about my nerves." Living as we do in cities, we lose the sense of personal worth and individual moral responsibility. We retreat into loneliness rather than face reality. In an economy like ours, with gadgets, comforts, and other material things, we feel no need for

God. W. A. Smart, in *The Contemporary Christ,* said, "We are talking not about people who deny the existence of God. . . . The point is not that they disbelieve in God, but that they can find nothing for him to do." We are directed by what everyone else is doing, by popular fashion, by public opinion. Books have been written on *The Hidden Persuaders, The Organization Man.* The world has invaded our souls, and we are not only in the world; we are of the world. And when the chips are down, there is nothing to sustain us.

There's a loneliness peculiar to young people. This is a feeling that no one understands. This calls for a separate sermon, and it may be found on page 94.

Then, there is the loneliness that death brings. Separation from our friends and members of our families makes us lonely. There is a natural wistfulness about the condition and state of our dear ones after death. Here is one area of life about which we know so little. Our loneliness is over separation. We grow accustomed to voices, a sense of security in wise counsel, and familiar faces around the table. Suddenly these are no more. And we feel cut off. Here is something we cannot share, at least not now. Death is a universal experience, and yet every man must do his own dying. None can share it with him. There is not just the loneliness that surges over us when our loved ones die, but for far too many there is the tragic loneliness of anticipating one's own death. We have much to learn about death and its meaning for us and for those we love. It produces loneliness.

The loneliness of age is a thing that disturbs many people. The psalmist said, "I looked on my right hand, and beheld, but there was no man that would know me: refuge failed me; no man cared for my soul" (Ps. 142: 4). Especially is loneliness a problem when people have been so busy making money, going and doing, that they have had little time to make friends or store up spiritual reserves against the coming of old age. We smile at the nursery rhyme,

> Old Mother Hubbard went to the cupboard
> To get her poor dog a bone.
> But when she got there, the cupboard was bare,
> And so the poor dog had none.

Barren cupboards are pressing spiritual matters when age begins to creep up on us and we find our reserves inadequate.

Rejected love produces loneliness. The counselor's office is filled with people who have tried to love, only to have it unreturned. Rejection is difficult to swallow. Some people cannot give love, and others cannot receive it. Love is never a right to be demanded. It cannot be bought or earned. It is a gift that is bestowed. To feel rejected creates a crisis, for it brings one's whole personality into question. It raises doubts about one's lovableness, or character, or personhood. People rejected feel lonely and often bring hurt to themselves and to those who have rejected them.

There is also the loneliness of leadership. I have felt

142

this as a minister. The leader must take the stand he believes to be right, regardless of what his followers or his congregation think. The minister can be the loneliest person on earth, even with the praise and adulation of an adoring congregation. Right is right, and the conscientious man must take his stand regardless. Through the years of racial crisis in our country, more than one minister has seen his congregation turn away from him, when he was doing the thing his conscience told him was right. The Christian congregation may not agree with the minister, but it ought always accord him the right of his opinion. This is what Joan was talking about in George Bernard Shaw's *Saint Joan:*

Yes, I am alone on earth. I have always been alone. Do not think that you can frighten me by telling me that I am alone. France is alone; and God is alone; and what is my loneliness before the loneliness of my country and my God? I see now that the loneliness of God is his strength; what would he be like if he listened to your jealous little counsels? Well, my loneliness shall be my strength, too; it is better to be alone with God: his friendship will not fail me, nor his counsel, nor his love. In his strength I will dare, and dare, and dare until I die.

Jesus knew this loneliness of leadership when he preached in his own hometown. People whispered among themselves, "Is not this Joseph's son?" He felt lonely when he realized the end of his earthly career was near, and that his disciples would desert him; but he said, "I am not alone. . . ."

143

Loneliness is at once a crisis and the possibility of greatness. It is almost an intolerable compliment that God has paid us. Every man must learn how to handle his aloneness. He must learn to live in it, and he must learn how to "leave" it.

There are other kinds of loneliness than these. We do many things to overcome loneliness—most of them superficial and more detrimental than helpful. We drink excessively, work furiously, go incessantly. We plan our schedules so that we are never alone, even though, as we saw earlier, this is never a cure for loneliness. I knew a young woman in college who would not even walk to the post office alone. Nor would she walk to the dining hall by herself. Excessive sex activities never provide an adequate answer to the problem, though in this relationship we give ourselves to another. Numerous coffee breaks, parties, hours before television, many civic and charitable activities—none of these of itself offers a cure for our loneliness.

There is an answer. It must be obvious by now. If our problem is an inner one, rather than an outer, then the answer lies in doing something about the inner life. Here are some possibilities.

Make friends with Jesus Christ. Earthly friendships are fickle things. Friends come and go. They leave us on a whim. We may feel the loneliness of rejected love, departing friends, lapse of morals, inward emptiness, but there is one constant companion who never forsakes us or leaves us: Jesus Christ. James Simpson, the Scottish surgeon, was asked what was the greatest dis-

144

covery he had ever made. He replied, "That Jesus Christ is my personal friend." The simplest definition of what it means to be a Christian is that we accept Jesus' offer of friendship and live the kind of life that enables us to keep faith with that friend. Friendship with Jesus is deeper than surface, and is never subject to changing times or moods. It does not exploit the object of friendship. It spends itself for the other. It goes on in spite of fault and failure. That friendship is a frank, unhesitating opening of heart and mind to each other. In the Dialogues of Buddha is this definition of a friend: "He guards you when you are off your guard and does not forsake you in trouble; he even lays down his life for your sake; he restrains you from doing wrong; he enjoins you to do right; he reveals to you the way to heaven." If this is true of earthly friendships, how much more is it true of our friendship with Jesus! Every kind of love can be shared with him. Every problem, every disappointment, every secret longing, can be discussed. He is the Friend who always does us good and never hurt. How do you make friends with Jesus? As you would with any other. You spend time in his presence, with the Bible, and in prayer. When you see him as he is, you give yourself to him. You accept his offer of friendship. You share thoughts and conversations. You do things for him, as he does things for you. Is not this the pattern of earthly friendships? Just so, it is the pattern of the heavenly Friendship!

Cultivate the fine art of solitude. Loneliness and solitude have been confused, they are not the same. Loneli-

ness can be transformed into creative solitude. This can
be done in a crowded trolley, or on a mountainside,
where Jesus was so often alone. The times when we
feel most alone are the times when we can best cultivate
the presence of God. Jesus was alone, but never lonely.
Faced with desertion, he said to his disciples, "I am not
alone, because the Father is with me." When he went to
the hills alone, he was not alone. He was earth's loneliest man in many ways. Rejected, despised, ill-treated,
he sought companionship with God. His loneliness was
not a morbid thing, nor did it make him neurotic. He
used it as a means of getting close to God. And this is
the highest way to transform our loneliness. When our
souls rise to God, we are transformed; our loneliness is
taken away, and it becomes possible for us to relate
ourselves to people in a creative and satisfying way. In
our solitude we have the presence of the Eternal. Solitude is the secret of productivity in life. The strong
people are those who know the kind of solitude Jesus
knew. The greatest psalm of them all was born in the
solitude of the Judean hills. What an affirmation of
faith it is: "The Lord is my Shepherd; I shall not want."

I said in the beginning that we can never reach the
innermost heart of another being. We are isolated from
each other, "islands." But in our communion with God
we can reach the innermost being of another person,
as Tillich says, "in a movement that rises first to God
and then returns from him to the other self. In this
way man's aloneness is not removed, but taken into the
community with that in which the center of all beings

146

rests, and so into community with all of them." This is why faith in God is so important in the family. The closer husband and wife get to God, the nearer they get to each other. The same applies to parent-child relationships, as to all others in life. In solitude, loneliness is transformed into creativity by the presence of God. We can be alone, and not be lonely!

We nourish our loneliness and feed it by concentrating our thoughts upon ourselves, our problems, our needs. Loneliness is not helped, by furious activity, by rushing around until we are exhausted. It is helped as we enter into the lives and experiences of other people, perhaps other lonely people. Someone made a survey a few years ago to discover what people do in trouble. One of the answers was, "Go to the movies and lose myself in somebody else's mess!" Here is an answer to loneliness. Lose yourself in somebody else's mess, and not in the movies but in actual living. Years ago John Bright, destined to hold a high post in the government of England under William Gladstone, lost his wife by death. He sat and brooded, lonely, dejected, grief-stricken. A friend, Richard Cobden, came to see him one day and said, "John, when this first wild surge of your sorrow is over, you and I will go through the streets of England and find millions of poor women suffering unfairly because of our unjust Corn Laws, and together you and I will throw ourselves into the job of repealing those laws!" This struck a sympathetic chord in John Bright's heart, and he went out and crusaded until the Corn Laws were repealed. He literally used his pain to strengthen his personality. And our loneliness is assuaged when we get concerned with other people, their loneliness, their needs, their ambitions.

Don't forget the fellowship of the church. Our friendship with Jesus needs to find a focus in an institution. The church is the redemptive fellowship—or should be. She is different from every other organization. With all her failings, there is none like her on earth. The lonely find a transforming solitude in worship hours. They find a fellowship that is concerned. Here are people who care. All of us need the experience of being able to say, "I belong." Here in a city, where the loneliest place may be the busiest place, there is help in the church. How sad it is for people to move to a big city and then become anonymous, "islands," lonely. And it is not necessary. The church stands with doors opening outward in welcome to all who come, offering a "tie that binds our hearts in Christian love."

Albert Camus, in *The Plague*, portrayed the longing loneliness in the human soul, and gave an answer. A city in North Africa had been isolated by a plague. No one had been allowed to enter or leave the city for some time. Hundreds of people died, and those who didn't die were sick and lonely. Christmas time came, and a man stood looking into a store window. There was despair in his face as he thought of his wife. He had not seen her for a long time, and he was not sure he would ever see her again. A doctor stood watching the old man peer into the window. He knew what was going on in the old man's mind. Camus wrote: "He knew what the old man was thinking as his tears flowed and thought it too: that a loveless world is a dead world, and always there comes an hour when one is weary of prisons, of one's work and devotion to duty, and all one craves for is a loved face, the warmth and wonder of a loving heart."

Ah, this is our feeling now. We, living in a world gone mad, where evil seems never to be conquered, where we are separated from those we love by distance or death, where loneliness in a dozen forms haunts us, long for a loved face. Ah, my beloved, know that God cares. In friendship with him, nourished by creative solitude and cultivated by doing his bidding, you will find that loneliness is transformed, and life becomes radiant, purposeful, and good.

"Woman, thou art loosed from thine infirmity."—Luke 13:12

What Can You Do with an Old
~~~~~~~~~~~~~~~~~~~~~~~~~~~~~Lead Sinker?

A fable from *The Arabian Nights* tells of two Persian merchants visiting the shop of a very poor tentmaker. One of them handed him a purse containing one hundred pieces of gold, saying, "Take this and start your fortune." The two merchants had had an argument about the best way to make a man rich. One of them had said, "In order to become wealthy, a man must have a certain amount of capital." The other insisted that a man must start with nothing and work up. They decided to settle the argument with the tentmaker.

Of course, the tentmaker was glad to get the gold. He was hungry, so he used ten pieces of gold to buy food and put the other ninety pieces in his turban. While he stood cooking his food, vultures flew low to steal the

150

meat. He fought with the birds and drove them off; but the claws of one caught in his turban, and the bird flew away with the turban and ninety pieces of gold.

The merchants came again, and the tentmaker told them of his battle with the vultures. They laughed heartily. The first merchant said, "I believe you. Here is another hundred pieces of gold." The tentmaker was determined that nothing should happen this time, so he hid the money in an old brass jar in the pantry. It had stood there for years undisturbed. Then he went out of town for a few days. While he was gone, a buyer of brass came through, and the tentmaker's wife found the old jar and sold it to him. When the merchants came back, he told them how the gold had slipped through his fingers once again. The first merchant turned to the other and said, "I will admit I was wrong; now let us try your theory." The second merchant gave the tent-maker an old lead sinker, saying, "Take this and start your fortune."

The tentmaker threw the old lead sinker on the shelf and forgot it. Later that day a fisherman came to town. He had lost the main sinker on his nets and was unable to go to sea until he could replace it. He promised his first catch of fish to anyone who could supply him a sinker. The tentmaker remembered the old lead sinker on the shelf and gave it to him. The first catch of fish was not large, but while cleaning one fish, the tent-maker's wife found a diamond. It was of no great value, but the tentmaker sold it for enough to buy material for a dozen tents. He sold these for enough to double the number, and gradually his shop grew into the greatest tentmaking factory in Persia.

How many of us feel that life has handed us an old lead sinker in one form or another! Nearly every person I know has a handicap. Not all handicaps are physical. Some are mental, some are emotional, some are spiritual. A bent back, a warped mind, a dwarfed soul—all are handicaps. Many a man has a perfect body but a not-so-perfect spirit. Some of our handicaps are born with us. Some come to us through accidents. Some we bring on ourselves by wrong living. Some are self-inflicted. All of us have a handicap of some kind. I have never known a man who was not dealing with handicaps in one way or another.

That is not important. It puts us in good company. Lincoln said once that the Lord must have loved the common man, he made so many of them. That is true of the handicapped man. There are so many of them. The important thing is to learn to handle and use a handicap. Many a man has let a bent back make him a grouch. Others with poor eyesight have become resentful and moody. A warped mind and a dwarfed spirit can make us temperamental and hard to live with. But when a handicap does this to us, the odds against us are more than doubled. Plenty of people complain and carp that life has given them a raw deal. This is poison to the whole body. Lord Byron had a club foot; it made him bitter. He was a great poet, but I have often wondered what he could have done if he had handled his handicap in a different way.

A person may have limitations; but when he decides to use his limitations and not let them use him and give him an inferiority complex, he becomes a better person and does better work. There is no dishonor in having a handicap. The dishonor comes in letting the handicap get the upper hand.

The world tends to pass by those who are handicapped, thus adding to their unhappiness. The world can be cruel, and for a man to make a mistake is to brand him forever in the eyes of people. Our standard of success is all wrong. We think a person must be physically perfect, have money, be the head in whatever his venture, be popular with the crowd, in order to be a success. Some of the people who get all these things are life's worst grouches! Some of them have taken their own lives, so unhappy did they become. The world was shocked by the death of Marilyn Monroe. Millions of girls throughout the country looked on her as the pinnacle of success. She had it! Money, fame, beauty—these are the goals of people all over the world. But having these things, she lacked the one thing without which life is utterly futile: happiness. She couldn't take all her other assets and turn them into this one. She was a huge success in the eyes of the world, but in her own eyes she was a hopeless failure!

Think about heaven. There are going to be some real surprises about who gets there and who doesn't. Some of the people who have received the adulation of the world will be amazed to hear the Saviour say, "Depart from me; I never knew you." And some who have thought themselves too lowly and small and humble will be amazed and gladdened to hear him say, "Thou hast been faithful over a few things; I will make thee ruler over many things. Enter thou the joy of thy Lord."

Take the story of the Pharisee and the tax collector. (Luke 18:10-14.) "Two men went up into the temple to pray; the one a Pharisee, and the other a publican." The Pharisee took his stand ostentatiously, and began to pray aloud: "God, I thank thee, that I am not as other men are, extortioners, unjust, adulterers, or even as this publican. I fast twice in the week, I give tithes of all that I possess."

But the tax collector, standing at a distance, would not even lift up his eyes to heaven, but kept striking his breast, saying, "God, be merciful to me a sinner." Jesus said, "I tell you, this man went down to his house justified rather than the other; for every one that exalteth himself shall be abased; and he that humbleth himself shall be exalted."

Success in life is to take what we have, do our best, and use it for the glory of God and to help other people. Whether our name is known outside this country is not important, but if we do these things, we are a huge success. The world tends to pass by the handicapped and the failure. Emerson once said that a weed is a flower that has never realized its possibilities. And in every man there is greatness. Don't undervalue any man.

Men do not arrive because the path is smooth. They arrive because they take what they have, add to that a

power greater than themselves, and set out to overcome and use whatever handicaps and limitations they
may have. We are defeated in mind and spirit and not
by obstacles. It is easy to think failure and get in the
rut of a failure complex. No man is defeated until he
gives in to defeat. The world has produced some people
of high success and courage from the handicapped.
Paul had a thorn in the flesh. We'll never know what it
was. Epilepsy and eye trouble have been guesses, but
no one knows. He called it a "messenger of Satan to
buffet me." He asked three times that it be taken away.
But instead he heard the voice of God saying to him,
"My grace is sufficient for thee" (II Cor. 12:9).

A library of books has been written by the handicapped. Milton was blind. Robert Louis Stevenson was
afflicted by tuberculosis. Sir Walter Scott was lame.
Alexander Pope was such an invalid that he had to be
sewed up in canvas every morning in order to stand at
all. Science has gone forward by the work of the handicapped. Charles Steinmetz was a hunchback. Teachers
told Thomas Alva Edison that he was too stupid to
learn.

In the world of politics no name shines brighter than
that of Franklin Delano Roosevelt, and yet he was a
polio victim. In the world of entertainment Walt Disney
was fired from a newspaper once because he had no
ideas and no talent.

The story of Louis Braille is a thrilling one. He was
only three years old when he was blinded. Born in
Coupvray, forty miles from Paris, he was the son of a

harness maker. When he was three, he was playing in his father's shop one day. He put the point of the awl on a strip of leather, as he had seen his father do, and hit the handle of the awl with the mallet. The point of the awl slipped and went into his eye. An infection set in; it soon spread to the other eye, and Louis Braille became totally blind.

His parents took him to a school in Paris for blind children. The methods of teaching the blind to read were clumsy and tedious, but Louis Braille learned. While he was still in his teens, he heard about a method of writing and reading using tiny pinpricks for letters. It was a method discovered by Charles Barbier. The idea caught Louis' imagination, and he set to work to perfect it. So the Braille alphabet came from the fertile mind of a blind boy. In 1829 the alphabet was first published. One hundred years later there was a celebration in Coupvray, the hometown of the man who had brought new life to countless thousands of blind people. A statue of Louis Braille was unveiled. Scores of blind people stood about the base of the statue; and as the drapery was removed, they stepped forward with upraised hands, moving their sensitive fingertips over the face of the man who had given them victory over darkness.

These are names known to us all. Many lesser ones whose names we may never hear have also triumphed over handicaps.

Men do not arrive because the path is smooth, but because they have determination to rise above handicaps, and because they learn to use them, and because they lay hold on a higher power that can help them. William Wordsworth in "Happy Warrior" sums it up when he talks of a man who, though

> . . . doomed to go in company with Pain,
> And Fear, and Bloodshed, miserable train!
> Turns his necessity to glorious gain;
> In face of these doth exercise a power
> Which is our human nature's highest dower.

Finally, consider some suggestions about overcoming and using handicaps.

Be absolutely honest with yourself. Our first reaction to a handicap in ourselves is rebellion or self-pity. Why should life hand me an old lead sinker? Why should I be thwarted in my desires to do some great and useful thing? Admit your handicap, whatever it is. If it is an inferiority complex, a physical deformity, a mental problem, an emotional problem, some deep sin, be perfectly honest about it. Face it. The ego does not like to be hurt, and we build up all kinds of defenses. There is no hope for any man until he can be honest with himself. The alcoholic can never get help until he comes to the point of saying, "I am an alcoholic. I am powerless over this thing. Only God can help me." When a man honestly faces the problem, there is no hopeless case. Say to yourself, this is my weakest point. And you can become strongest right here. They tell us that when intense heat is applied to metal in welding, the welded joint becomes stronger than the parent metal. In a furniture factory a man glues two pieces of wood together, then applies intense heat and pressure, and the glued joint is stronger than the original board. Your weakest point may become your greatest strength. Be honest about your handicap. Don't hide it or be ashamed of it. Be ashamed only when you let it get the best of you! Harry Emerson Fosdick tells of the time when Ole Bull, the violinist, was playing a concert in Paris. His A string snapped, but he transposed the composition and finished on three strings. This happens. To face a broken A string honestly, accept it, do something with what is left—that is living.

Use your handicap. No matter what yours is, there are ways to use it to good advantage for the glory of God. In the Norton Art Gallery at West Palm Beach, Florida, there is a magnificent collection of Chinese jade. These pieces of jade have been worked into designs of great beauty. Green predominates, but there are other colors; such as blue, amber, and white. One of the most beautiful of all is cut in brown relief against a white background. It was made from a piece of jade with a deep flaw in it. Some wise Chinese artist saw the possibilities in this faulty stone and carved it into a thing of rare beauty. This can happen to flaws in physical makeup, handicaps of the mind or the emotions. What seems to be a useless thing and a real drawback can be transformed into something of use and beauty. Arthur E. Gordon lay in an iron lung in a hospital in Cincinnati. He said that all he could think of was his sad condition. Then one day he got an idea. Why not make the iron lung a pulpit? So he had little plaques made and pasted over the lung. That first day he told the therapist that God loved her. This went on and on. After two years he was using a portable respirator and a wheelchair, but still using these for a pulpit. Gordon said that during the thirteen months of hospitalization he led fifteen people to Christ. His handicap became a radiant pulpit!

Roy L. Smith once wrote:

Any person who is attempting to lighten the load which is breaking the hearts of other people is very likely to forget his own load. It is a strange thing, but true, that as we lift the burdens of other people we find our own growing lighter. Some of the happiest people you will ever meet are the burden bearers who have slipped out from under their own griefs long enough to bear the griefs of others.

Grace Noll Crowell tells of an American soldier on weekend leave who stood on a bleak, foggy corner in London, homesick. Suddenly from a basement window came a burst of bird song so clear and sweet that he was transported back to his home in the southern United States. He was hearing again the mockingbird in the magnolia tree in the garden. It couldn't be a mockingbird in the basement. He went down to see. A tailor was seated at his bench. "What can I do for you, sir?" the tailor asked. "You can tell me where you learned to whistle so beautifully and what is the inspiration," the soldier said. There was a smile on the tailor's lips. "From an aching leg. You see, I picked up a bit of shrapnel in the last war, and my leg seldom gives me much ease." "But the music was filled with light—and gladness." "Why not?" asked the tailor. "Gladness and light are all about us if we have the eyes to see them, and pain should not blind us to them. I have often thought that a sufferer knows more of the essence of joy than do the free ones. At any rate one may as well whistle as to complain. It really takes less energy." "And yet you are able to send out hope and inspiration to the men above in the street!" said the soldier. "Pain usually does something to one. It makes a person break silence. Whistling has become a sort of habit with me, and I whistle when my leg forgets to ache as well as when it is at its worst. Surely folks like to listen to it better than if I groaned all the while." "Indeed they do, sir!" said the boy. "You have heartened me more than I can say. I came down here feeling mighty discouraged, and I am going away much better. Thank you for helping me."

One way for the handicapped to save themselves is to give themselves in service. In fact, this applies to everybody, and not just the handicapped. Alfred Adler says of children: "Only a child who desires to contribute to the whole, whose interest is not centered in himself, can train successfully to compensate for defects. If children desire only to rid themselves of difficulties, they will continue backward." Jesus knew the truth when he said, "Whosoever will save his life shall lose it; but whosoever shall lose his life . . . shall save it" (Mark 8:35).

Put your life completely in the hands of Jesus Christ. Religious faith is a powerful medicine. It may not take away the handicap if it is physical or mental, but faith in him gives us the power to use the handicap, whatever it is. Our Bible lesson is a story told by a doctor. A woman had suffered from a bent back for eighteen years. Of course it had caused her pain. It must have been embarrassing too. The doctor tells us that she had more than a bent back; she had a "spirit of infirmity." Her back was bent, but this other thing had got the best of her. Her spirit was warped too. She may have had a good case of self-pity. At any rate she did not have the joy she should have had in living. But the doctor tells us that this woman met Jesus, and he said to her, "Woman, thou art loosed from thine infirmity." The most important thing he did for her was not to straighten her back, but to loose her from the spirit of infirmity. Her handicap had made life miserable. Now she was loosed from the power of the handicap, and even if Jesus had not straightened her back, she would have been a well, whole woman.

This always happens. Sometimes faith in Jesus can remove the handicap itself. Sometimes it is physical or mental and cannot be cured in this life. But Jesus can take away the power of the handicap over us and give us power to rise above it and use it for his glory and for the glory of mankind. Samuel Rutherford was in prison in Aberdeen once. Something happened to him, and he described it this way: "Jesus Christ came into

161

my room last night and every stone shone like a ruby!"
This happens to our handicaps when we submit ourselves completely to him. We may go on through life
with a bent back; but Christ can give us inner power
and radiance, and we can be happy regardless of the
circumstances. If your handicap is a great sin, or a
small one, Christ takes it away when you surrender to
him. If it is an emotional problem, he brings health. I
am about to decide that a religious faith is the best
help for emotional problems. God is concerned with a
speck like you and me! We matter to him, for he made
us. When we bring our infirmities and our handicaps to
him, he heals us. He does what is best for us. And
though he may not heal a bent back or a crooked foot,
he can do something more important than that. He can
heal a bent spirit and a crooked soul! Paul was right
when he said, "If any man be in Christ, he is a new
creature" (II Cor. 5:17). Here are three helps in transforming handicaps to usefulness: Be honest about it;
use your handicap; but above all else, submit yourself
to Jesus Christ.

"The last enemy that shall be destroyed is death."
—I Cor. 15:26

As Soon as a Man Is Born, He Is Old
Enough to Die

We have been considering the theme, When Crisis Comes. Before we close the book, I want us to think on this sentence: "To be really proficient in the art of living, we must know and understand something about dying." Death is a stage in life; dying is an important factor in it. Death is passing from one experience, one part of life, to another. To be a whole person, one must have an adequate philosophy of death.

We moderns have lost the horizon of eternity. In our blindness we say a lot of foolish things, things which may sound sophisticated but which are really stupid when analyzed. H. L. Mencken, for example, said that he had no desire for immortality. He added that it was the childish belief of inferior men. I began thinking about some of the inferior men who have certainly believed in immortality: Socrates, Plato, Spinoza, Wesley, Moody. Alfred Lord Tennyson, one of the greatest of the English poets, believed it. Listen:

> Thou wilt not leave us in the dust:
>   Thou madest man, he knows not why,
>   He thinks he was not made to die;
> And thou hast made him: thou art just.

Robert Ingersoll, who most of his life had been a professed atheist, came down to the death of a loved one, and this is what he said:

Life is a narrow veil between the cold and barren peaks of two eternities. We strive in vain to look beyond the heights: We cry aloud and the only answer is the echo of our wailing cry. From the voiceless lips of the unreplying dead there comes no word: But in the night of death, Hope sees a star, and listening Love can hear the rustle of a wing.

These men have seen beyond the shadows of this earth, and their eyes have dimly seen the light of another life that is to be. There is something about modern doubt that is chilling and cold. Doubt withers a personality. There is something about a faith that is like the sun—it makes things grow and thrive. We moderns have lost faith in immortality; and, as a consequence, we grope in darkness. We accuse our fathers of being too otherworldly. We are too this-worldly.

Let's take a moment to look at some attitudes toward death and the life after death.

There is a strong feeling today that life is futile and that we are working at something that doesn't matter. Every last one of us would like to be convinced of the importance of living, but when we measure life by number of days only, we find there isn't much to it. How fast the threescore years and ten glide by! How many people there are gripped by a sense of personal insignificance—an inferiority complex in the face of the bigness of the universe. Much of this feeling is due to the fact that we have lost sight of eternity and have tried to define life in terms of the here and now alone. We live from day to day, hand to mouth, saying that when the future comes, then we'll take care of that. But every man needs something solid under his feet upon which to build—something lasting, which is the same yesterday, today, and forever. And we have the feeling that our trust in this life only isn't enough. It all looks so hopeless and so futile and so temporary.

Others try to ignore death. It is foolish to fail to realize that those whom we love most dearly we hold only by a slender thread that can be broken in a moment. One of the tragic things I see in my work is a family that has acted as though its members would live forever, making no preparation against the inevitable coming of death. They have built up no sustaining faith in a future life, or in the goodness of life, or in the goodness of God, but have simply lived life from day to day without reference to the Eternal. Too many

165

of the more fortunate in this life ignore the claims of death and live with the attitude that it happens to everybody else but not to them. But it happens to all of us. In our youth we like to think of ourselves as living and not dying. Others die; the old die; our friends die. But not us. Even in our youth we ought to think seriously about the day of our passing from life to life. Adelaide Crapsey wrote in "Verse":

> Why have
> I thought the dew
> Ephemeral when I
> Shall rest so short a time, myself,
> On earth?

When we are young, in the springtime of life, we think little of the coming of age or fall. But in the middle of life we begin to hear the locust sing, and we are reminded that winter and frost are not far away.

Other people think it is our job to build here an earthly paradise and forget about living hereafter. The attempt to build a paradise on earth has been long and noble. Much good has been done. Life has been made better. Its span has been lengthened. Disease has been conquered, and the greatest blessings in this conquest of disease lie yet ahead. Some say, "Lengthen this life; give me a few more years, and a few more things, and then let me go!" This is a direct quotation from a man approaching old age. Life is not something to measure in years and things. When we have lived the longest number of years and have amassed the greatest number of things, there is still something in the human heart that hungers and thirsts.

Still others think that to believe in life after death is to destroy a man's desire to do something worthwhile here and now. And I suppose at this point religion does become an opiate for some people. They are willing to let things alone as they are, and wait for the pie in the sky by and by. Two preachers were asked to help with a drive to do something in one of our large cities. They replied that they didn't have time; they were too busy getting ready for heaven and helping others get ready. Some think that to destroy the idea of immortality would make men devote their energies to making this world better. Not so. When we forget that we are creatures of eternity, we can do horrible things to our brothers. This world has been going from bad to worse since we took our eyes off the idea of immortality. To believe in life after death does something to the way we live here and now. When Henry David Thoreau lay dying, Parker Pillsbury sat by his side and said, "Henry, you are so near the border now, can you see anything on the other side?" Thoreau replied, "One world at a time!" Many think this.

Modern moods of doubt and denial do not satisfy. A British scientist believes that at death the spirit of man will be extinguished like a candle flame. Many people think death ends all. I firmly believe that the increase in crime in our country is directly due to the fact that we no longer believe in immortality. We see nothing divine in man. He is an animal. The Communists teach that man is a machine, and when the machine is worn out, there is nothing wrong with destroying it. We can steal and cheat and kill and rape because we do not see in man that something that lives forever! Scientists today are talking more and more about God and immortality. What we know of God, what we know of value, what we know of man, will not let us think that a person just lies down and dies.

Still others say they will not believe something they cannot prove. I talked with a man last week who insisted that I could not prove anything about life after death. Scientifically I couldn't. But then I asked him to prove that there is no such thing. He didn't know where to begin. Be careful when you say you won't believe anything you can't prove. You can't live a day on that basis. What is love? Explain a kiss between two lovers. We trust the banker, the druggist, the postman. But when we come to matters of religion, we say we won't believe it because we can't prove it. Many men insist that we must accept the fact of death. So we must. They go on to say that we must adjust ourselves to thinking that death is the very end. To which I shout, "No, we must not!" It is not a matter of a choice between facts and faith. It is a choice between faiths. I choose the faith that best suits my needs. I believe in immortality with a strong and steady conviction. As Martineau put it, "We do not believe in immortality because we can prove it, but we try to prove it because we cannot help believing it." I believe that when I pass from this life there is another life where certain things will be true, and in a moment I want us to look at them.

Bishop Gerald Kennedy tells of a man who left his career, gave up his family and everything, and became a beachcomber on a far-off Pacific island. He tried to forget his past and to be satisfied to live out his remaining years as a derelict. He did everything he could to kill memory and destroy hope. But something kept reminding him that he was made for more than that, that he was not what he ought to be. He could not forget his gifts, his education, his family. He solved no problems by trying to run from life. He became unhappier than before.

I think this is our trouble: We will not find faith, and we cannot be happy with doubt. We are not willing to seek God as if we had to find him, but we cannot sell our souls and be happy about it. Without faith in something more than the life we now have, we are like a man trying to build a bridge on one pillar. Men in prison camps during the war developed "barbed-wire sickness." It was not something that could be treated by a doctor. It was of the mind and spirit. The same kind of sickness takes hold on humankind when we try to content ourselves with the boundaries of this present life and set them up as final and absolute. Men get sick, for the temporal is not their natural living place. Men were born with eternity in their hearts, and to deny it is to be unhappy. We are made for long views and far horizons. This life is neither the end nor an end. It is a beginning.

The greatest thinking about life after death can be summed up in the Resurrection of Jesus. The heart of the Christian message is that the power of God raised him from the dead and that he is alive forevermore. The early disciples didn't know how it was done or what happened. Neither do we, and speculation about it is futile. It was done. The Resurrection explains the Christian message. There is no substitute for it in our gospel. When we try to explain it away, there is always a loophole in our argument. Paul didn't talk of Jesus' teachings, he talked of the Resurrection. The Resurrection has become the point on which we stand to see life in its true perspective. Jesus took the sting out of death. His Resurrection was his way of saying to all who should come after him, "I have been there. I know. Follow me." Paul pointed to the same fact when he said, "Death is swallowed up in victory. O death, where is thy sting? O grave, where is thy victory?" He went on to say, "Thanks be to God, which giveth us the victory." And he says to us today, "therefore, my beloved brethren, be ye steadfast, unmoveable, always abounding in the work of the Lord." Life cannot be explained apart from a firm faith in immortality. If we have hope in Christ for this life only, then we are of all men most miserable. Christ died not just to make this life better, but to show his beloved the way to the place prepared for them.

In *Lazarus Laughed,* Eugene O'Neill tells how

170

Lazarus was raised from the dead by Jesus. Lazarus left home and went to Greece. In Athens he met the half-crazy, cruel Gaius Caligula, successor to the emperor Tiberius. Spies had told Caligula that the people hated him. He replied, "Let them hate—so long as they fear us! We must keep death dangling before their eyes! . . . I like to watch men die." This monster was confronted by Lazarus. Caligula accused Lazarus of teaching people to laugh at death and threatened him with execution. But Lazarus looked into his face, laughed softly, and answered, "Death is dead, Caligula!"

We know very little about life after death, but I want to share my convictions with you.

In the first place, what we consider death does not in any way affect the continuity of the individual's life. What we call death Jesus did not call death at all; he called it sleep. In his teaching death is something awful. He means the death of the soul, not of the body. "The soul that sinneth, it shall die." (Ezek. 18:20.) The body is not the important thing. It is only a temporary house for that which is eternal in us: the soul. We have forever. The passing days are not hastening us to our doom; they are leading us to a fuller life, greener pastures. Death is not to be feared, but looked upon as an experience that opens up to us greater perfection, purer joy, nobler happiness. Many people fear death; they have not availed themselves of the power that puts death in its true perspective in life. Or it may be that they would not want the qualities of their life here to be carried over into another life. When death comes to

171

a person who is ready, it is as natural as lying down to sleep. Something beautiful happens. Fear and horror disappear from faces as men are loosed from the clay that has bound them to the temples of God. We have no exact information about what is to follow death, and we have a wistful feeling as we carry our loved ones to a quiet resting-place. But I have a conviction that, because of what I know of God, death does not in any way affect the continuity of life.

In the second place, the deepest longings and desires of our souls shall be satisfied. Recall the comforting words in Rev. 7:16. "They shall hunger no more, neither thirst any more." What kind of hunger and thirst? Of the body? No, of the soul. The deepest and most sincere desires of our lives shall be fulfilled. We want things here that we cannot have. I have never preached the perfect sermon. You have never built the perfect house. You have never made the perfect pie. None of us have ever been as good or as kind as we want to be. We've never been able to serve our Lord as we feel we ought. Perfection is beyond us. We have a desire to be things that we cannot be here. These desires shall be fulfilled.

The thing that bothers us most is this: Will I see and know my loved ones? We have all stood and watched our loved ones die. We have asked, Shall we see them again? This is a normal desire. In the course of living together for a long number of years human lives become close. The sound of a voice becomes precious. The touch of a hand, a smile, the sound of a footstep—these become familiar and loved things. And death comes. Is that all? We need to learn that those we love will go from us. But is that the end?

Arthur John Gossip lost his wife in the 1920's. In 1929 he wrote a book and dedicated it to her: "To my wife— my daily comrade still." In 1945 he wrote another book and dedicated it to her also: "To my wife—now a long time in the Father's House." Does death end such comradeship? No, my friends, it does not. A prominent woman came to her preacher. She was past middle age. She had a difficult problem. She had been to several doctors, and all had told her that unless she had an operation, she could not live. Of course, they told her, if she had the operation, she might not get well. Her problem was this: A year before, her son had been killed in the war. She showed the preacher his picture. "I ask you, sir, if I die as a result of this operation, will I see him again?" She wanted the truth, and the preacher looked her straight in the eye and said, "It is my firm belief, based on what I know of Jesus Christ, that you will see him again." She thought a moment and then said, "How soon after I go?" The preacher said, "If your son was in a far country and you went to see him, you would look for him as soon as the boat landed, wouldn't you? The same applies here. You'll find him. It can't be long, for love never loses its own." She was satisfied. She had the operation. She did not live. She is with her son in the Father's house.

There will be continuity of life, fulfillment of personal longings; we shall see our loved ones; but one thing more: Heaven will be an adventure, a place of growth. Halford Luccock used to write a column for *The Christian Century* called "Simeon Stylites." Once he described a man who was always behind in his work because he had much to do. He never caught up. One night before he went to bed he thought to himself, "If only once for 20 minutes in 20 years I could catch up with myself!" He went to sleep and dreamed. He was in a great room with a mahogany desk, but there was not a single piece of paper on the desk. He saw out the window that the car was washed, the lawn mowed, the house freshly painted. There were no bills waiting to be paid. He had no engagements written on the calendar for the day. He had caught up with himself at last. He saw the postman go by, but there was no mail for him. Then the man asked, "Where am I?" The postman replied, "This is hell."

Heaven is not a place of stagnation, of nothing to do, but a place of adventure and growth and development in ways undreamed of. Did not Paul say, "Eye hath not seen, nor ear heard, neither have entered into the heart of man, the things which God hath prepared for them that love him" (I Cor. 2:9).

There is no logic by which I can prove what I have said to you. I say it because of what I personally know about Jesus. Only you yourself can convince yourself of immortality. It is not done by proposition or demonstration. But I know that those who die in the Lord are in the hands of a God of love; and what more could we ask? The process of birth holds a suggestion of what

I mean. An infant, snuggled up under the mother's heart during the prenatal days, is surrounded by warmth and protection. Suppose he could reason. He might say, "I don't want to be born. I don't want to go out of this world that I know into one that I don't know. I am happy here. I am afraid of birth." He might regard birth as we regard death. But then he is born, and looking down upon him is the sweetest face in the world. He is cuddled in his mother's arms, protected and fed and loved. God made it that way. After many years, the man comes to die. Need he be terrified at the prospect? If he had the love of God at birth, shall he not also have it at death? Can we not trust the same God to care for us in death that cared for us at birth?

I cannot tell you about the Father's house. I don't know. I do know that those prepared to live with the Father shall be surrounded by his love and care when the time comes to leave this familiar life. There is no need to fear. Only trust. All that I have said is pointless unless you decide to live for Jesus and begin now. Wilfred Grenfell, writing from aboard a small hospital ship of which he was captain, said, "I live in a world where preconceived opinions are at a discount. What interests me is what is to be done about a thing." What are you going to do to make preparation for dying? What is your response to the Resurrection? Is it just a beautiful but fanciful story to you? You can experience the power and hope of the Resurrection in your own life right now, and so be ready for that day when you pass from life to life. Eternal life really has its beginning now. Did not Jesus say it in simple words: "Whosoever liveth and believeth in me shall never die"? Live and believe in him, and death will have no terrors for you. Now, in health and good days, give him your heart, serve him with all your might, trust him like a child, and then one day you too can say, "Go down, death"!